REKINDLE THE LOVE

Discover The Secrets Guide and Strategies To Strengthen How To Fight For Your Marriage

By

Dr Becky Day

TABLE OF CONTENT

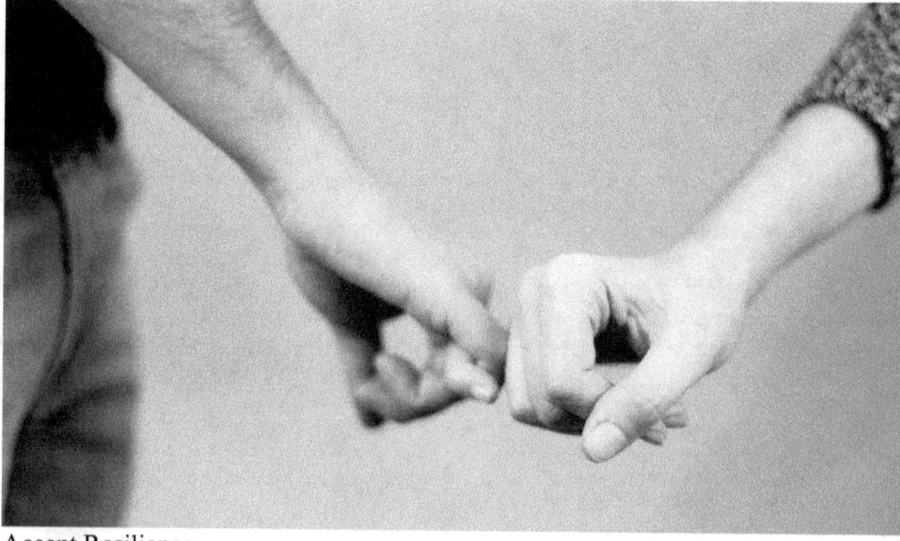

Prioritize Communication

Welcome Change Together
Practice Active Listening

Consistency in Actions

INTRODUCTION

Sarah and Michael lived once upon a time in the picturesque village of Willow Brook, a couple whose love had faded over the years.

They were once profoundly in love, but the routine of daily living had taken its toll.

However, fate had other plans to renew their love.

Sarah was browsing around the town's small bookstore on a bright afternoon when she came across a dusty old book with a faded cover that drew her eye.

The title, "The Magic of Love," piqued her interest, and she decided to buy it, thinking it would bring some excitement back into her life.

Sarah discovered a world of ancient knowledge on love, passion, and the skill of keeping a relationship alive as she read the book. The author, Sage Willow, a wise and enigmatic woman, provided stories and counsel that Sarah found extremely moving.

She was attracted by stories about couples overcoming obstacles and reigniting the embers of their love.

Sarah recommended they read the book together, eager to share her newfound expertise with Michael.

Michael, initially skeptical, agreed to give it a go in the hopes of injecting some much-needed enchantment into their relationship.

As they read the book together, the couple began to open up to one other in ways they hadn't in years.

The stories in the book functioned as a mirror, reflecting their difficulties and providing advice on how to overcome them.

They smiled at the funny stories and cried at the sad ones, understanding they were not alone in their troubles.

Sarah and Michael were inspired by the book and began integrating the principles into their own life.

They rediscover the pleasures of spending quality time together, valuing communication, and discovering new methods to show their love.

The book served as a catalyst for good transformation, rekindling a flame that had faded over time.

Sarah and Michael felt a renewed feeling of connectedness as the days passed. They went on impromptu vacations, discussed hopes and goals, and, most significantly, fell in love all over again.

The book had done its work, reminding them that love, like a flame, required nourishment and attention in order to burn brightly.

In the end, Sarah and Michael recognized that the actual beauty of love was found in ordinary moments shared between two people who were dedicated to developing together, rather than spectacular gestures or lavish displays.

The tattered and battered old book became a treasured keepsake— a remembrance of the adventure that had reignited their love and brought them closer than ever before. And so, Sarah and Michael lived happily ever after in the charming village of Willowbrook, armed with the timeless knowledge that had rescued their love.

Don't let your marriage dissolve into the mists of everyday existence.

Take charge of your love journey right now!

"Rekindle the Love and Discover the Secrets Guide" is your road map to a strong and happy marriage.

Grab your book and embark on a journey to reignite the flames, strengthen your relationship, and fight for the love you both deserve.

You're happily ever after begins right here!

ORDER A COPY NOW

 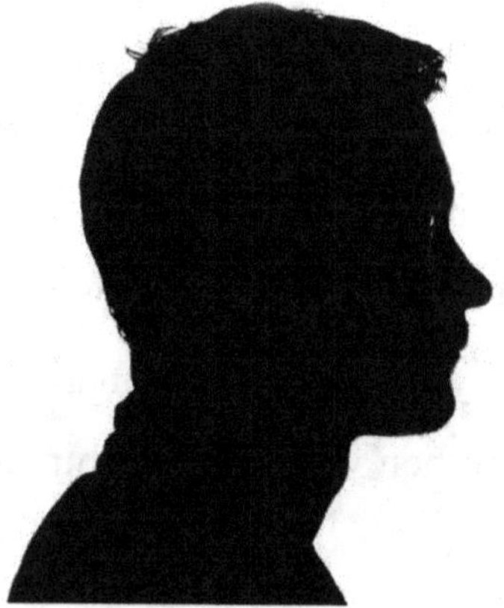

BOOK DESCRIPTION

Discover new ways that will help you and your relationship to emerge stronger and more connected than before.
No matter the hurdles that have come between you, this book offers you with the tools to repair trust, rekindle passion, and renew your commitment to a flourishing and enduring partnership.

Communicate with honesty and empathy, establishing deep understanding and connection. Navigate disagreements constructively, changing them into opportunities for growth.Cultivate closeness and reignite the physical and emotional sparks in your marriage.Build resilience to survive life's trials, emerge indestructible. Embrace the power of forgiveness and let go of past scars, paving the way for a brighter future.

Create a shared vision for your marriage, ensuring that your love story endures.

"Rekindle the Love" is not simply a book; it's a guide for people determined to conserving and developing the love they hold dear. The moment to fight for your marriage is now, and this book is your ally in that war.

If you're ready to rekindle the flame and develop a marriage that can weather anything, then this is the handbook you've been waiting for.

Your love story deserves a happy ending, and this book will teach you the way.

The "Rekindle the Love and Discover the Secrets Guide" is an enlightening booklet that will reinvigorate your marriage while also setting you on a road of personal growth and improvement.

This book is your compass in a world full of diversions and obstacles to reignite the flames of desire and strengthen the link that attracted you together in the first place.

Marriage is an elegant dance, and all relationships, no matter how strong, go through storms.

"Rekindle The Love" shines a light on the route to greater love, communication, and endurance.

Learn what seasoned couples do to stay together throughout difficult times and emerge stronger.

Discover the underlying sources of your relationship's stress.

To increase comprehension, master the skill of effective communication.

Rekindle passion with simple but powerful gestures; learn tried-and-true tactics for negotiating disagreements and emerging stronger. Rediscover the joy of friendship and shared goals.

In this book **you will discover the following**

Importance of Strengthening Your Marriage

Foundation of a Strong Marriage

Common Challenges Faced in Marriage

Reigniting the Spark in Your Marriage

Communication Strategies

Effective Communication Skills

Overcoming Communication Barriers

Understanding the Importance of Fighting for Your Relationship

Rebuilding Trust

Do you really want to know how to fight for your marriage to last longer that will give you a peace of mind? "If your answer is YES to this question, then search no further"

Click the Purchase Button let me assist you with a portion of my Fruitful aides

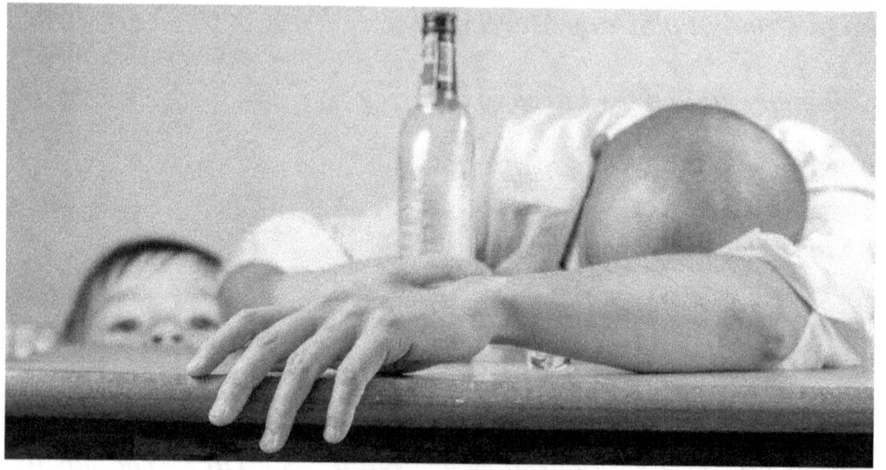

CHAPTER ONE

DEFINING THE BATTLEFIELD MODERN CHALLENGES IN MARRIAGE

Marriage, a timeless institution that has weathered the storms of history, today stands at the forefront of the modern battlefield of relationships.

It is a holy tie, a union built in love, trust, and dedication, yet it finds itself navigating through new ground in the 21st century.

As we embark on this journey together, we delve into the core of contemporary marriage, where fresh problems and complexities question the very essence of what it is to be married.

In a world that is always evolving, the dynamics of marriage have evolved as well.

The difficulties that couples confront now are different from those of our parents and grandparents.

The introduction of technology, altering gender roles, financial demands, and the ever-increasing pace of life have added unique challenges into the marital arena.

In this book, we will investigate these problems, deconstructing the elements that undermine the integrity of modern marriages while proposing techniques and answers to enhance the sacred bond.

"Defining the Battlefield: Modern Challenges in Marriage" is not just a compendium of common wisdom or a reiteration of age-old advice.

It offers a serious assessment of the specific problems and tribulations that contemporary couples experience daily.

This book is a guide to navigating the battlefield of modern marriage, offering thoughts, strategies, and real-world examples that will help you not just survive but thrive in your marital journey.

As we embark on this exploration, we will delve into the intricacies of communication in the digital era, the delicate balance of personal and shared goals, and the skill of sustaining intimacy among the chaos of the modern world.

We will address the impact of societal expectations, the role of uniqueness within a marriage, and the enduring power of love.

Ultimately, the issues that modern couples confront should not be perceived as insurmountable obstacles but as chances for growth, understanding, and perseverance.

This book is a monument to the enduring power of love and the ability of the human spirit to adapt, grow, and prosper in the face of tragedy.

So, fasten your seat belts and prepare to embark on a tour across the complicated battlefield of modern marriage.

In the pages that follow, we will explore the struggles, successes, and transforming moments that define this particular era of matrimony.

Together, we will unearth the keys to not just fighting for your marriage but also emerging victorious, hand in hand, in this current world of love, commitment, and relationship.

THE RESILIENCE OF LOVE:WHY YOUR MARRIAGE IS WORTH THE FIGHT

In the midst of life's chaos, with all its challenges and tribulations, it's tempting to question whether the battle to preserve and develop your marriage is worth the effort.

There are moments when the weight of your common past and the promise of a brighter future seem like simple illusions, dissipating like mist in the face of hardship. But it is precisely during these moments of doubt and despair that the genuine tenacity of love reveals itself.

Love, the driving force that brought you together, is an exceptional and enduring emotion.

It's the foundation upon which your marriage was built, and it has the strength to weather the fiercest storms.

Love is not a passive sentiment; it is an active energy that, when cultivated and fostered, can conquer the most daunting challenges.

In the chapters that follow, we will explore the reasons why your marriage is worth the fight, why the problems, arguments, and sacrifices are investments rather than losses.

We will look into the incredible potential of love to adapt, change, and endure.

Through the stories of innumerable couples who have overcome their own challenges and emerged stronger on the other side, we will discover inspiration and wisdom.

Your marriage is not just a pledge; it is a living, breathing organism that develops and evolves with you.

The conflicts you confront are not evidence of weakness but opportunities for growth, understanding, and connection.

In the face of modern circumstances, love is not a frail flower; it is a robust tree, securely established and capable of withstanding the hardest winds.

As we study the tenacity of love, we will find the underlying reasons why your marriage is worth every ounce of effort you invest. From the little, everyday gestures of kindness to the monumental moments of forgiveness and reconciliation, love thrives in the fertile soil of dedication, patience, and understanding. So, if you've ever questioned whether your marriage is worth the fight, join us on this journey of discovery.

Together, we will explore the reasons why love endures, and why, after all the hardships and tribulations, your marriage remains a source of unlimited strength, joy, and fulfillment.

The challenges you confront are not obstacles; they are chances to celebrate the enduring power of love.

NAVIGATING YOUR PATH TO VICTORY

Navigating one's route to triumph and rekindling one's love life are two interwoven components that greatly contribute to personal fulfillment and pleasure. Individuals frequently face problems, setbacks, and periods of stasis in their life's path.

Understanding how to overcome these challenges while also reigniting passion and love in many facets of life, on the other hand, may lead to a more satisfying and triumphant lifestyle.

HOW TO FIND YOUR WAY TO VICTORY

Define Your Objectives and Purpose

Before going on any trip, it is critical to set your objectives and comprehend your purpose. Clearly defined objectives serve as a road map, directing your efforts and decisions toward a successful conclusion. Consider both short-term and long-term objectives that are in line with your interests and beliefs.

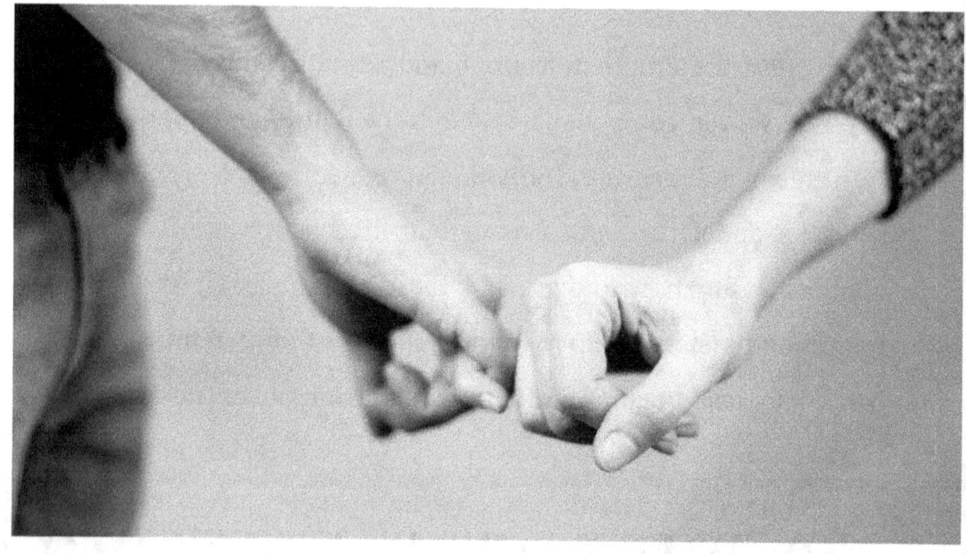

Accept Resilience

The ability to recover from adversity is referred to as resilience. Develop resilience by viewing setbacks as chances for progress. Learn from mistakes, adjust to changes, and have an optimistic attitude. Resilience enables you to meet challenges head-on and overcome hardship with grace.

Ongoing Learning and Improvement

Personal development and flexibility are enhanced by a dedication to lifelong learning.
Maintain your curiosity, seek new knowledge, and be open to learning new abilities.
The ability to adapt guarantees that you are more able to handle ever-changing terrain, enhancing your chances of success.

Create a Supportive Network

Surround yourself with people who will inspire and encourage you. A solid support system encourages you during difficult times and celebrates your triumphs.
Make relationships with like-minded people, mentors, and friends who can help you on your quest.

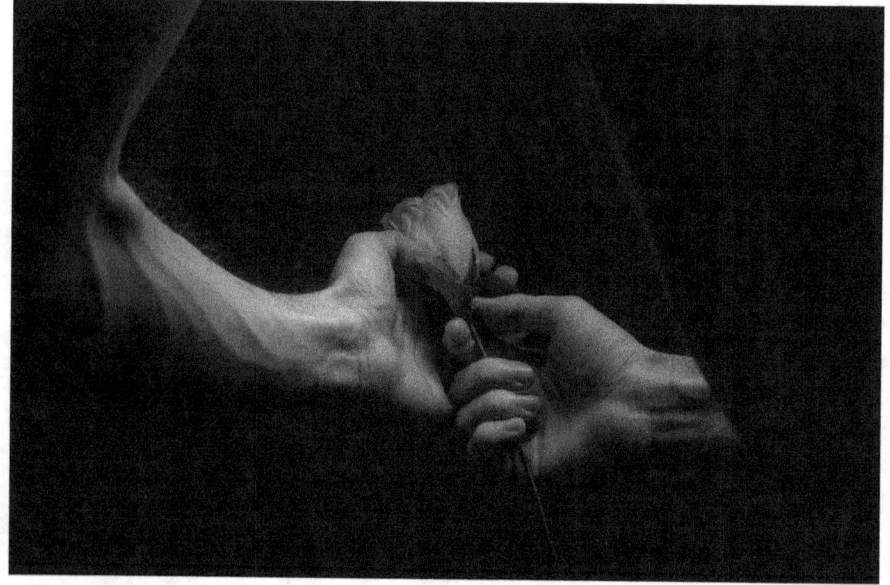

Thoughtful Decision-Making

Use awareness when making decisions. Consider your principles and the potential repercussions of your decisions, and make decisions that correspond with your aims.

REKINDLING THE PASSION

Love and Care for oneself

Begin by developing a strong feeling of self-love and practicing self-care. Prioritize your physical and emotional well-being.
Be kind with yourself and take stock of your abilities.
When you love and care for yourself, you are more able to love and care for others.

Communication and Relationship

Effective communication and true connection are the foundations of strong partnerships. Rekindle the passion in your relationships by encouraging open and honest conversation.
Share your views and feelings with people, actively listen to them, and try to comprehend their points of view.

Developing a deep emotional bond revitalizes love and intimacy.

Create Shared Experiences

Nurture love by sharing experiences and memories with those you care about. These experiences, whether through travel, common hobbies, or spending time together, build the link and add to a sense of togetherness.

Rediscover Your Passion and Adventure

Infuse your life with passion and adventure.
Try new things together, embrace spontaneity, and pursue similar hobbies to rekindle the flame. Rediscovering the thrill and joy in life keeps relationships and love fresh.

Forgiveness and Release

To reignite love, it is necessary to exercise forgiveness and let go of old grudges. Holding on to bitterness might make it difficult to connect emotionally. Accept forgiveness, both for yourself and for others, and cultivate a restored feeling of love and understanding.

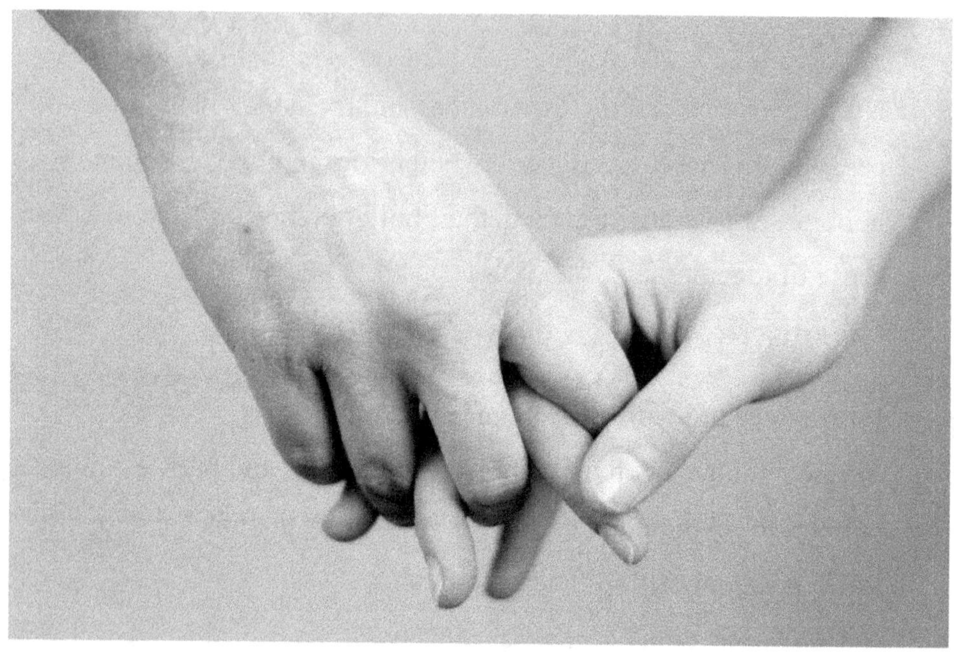

Conclusion

Navigating your way to triumph and rekindling the love in your life are both transformative experiences.

You prepare the route for success and fulfillment by defining clear goals, embracing resilience, and cultivating meaningful connections.

Simultaneously, you may breathe fresh life into relationships and rediscover the profound beauty of love via self-love, good communication, and shared experiences.

These factors, when combined, form a comprehensive strategy for living a triumphant and love-filled life.

FORTIFYING THE FOUNDATIONS

In the complex fabric of marriage, it is crucial to prioritize the establishment of a solid foundation to sustain a long-lasting and satisfying partnership.

The "Rekindle The Love and Discover the Secrets" guide provides essential knowledge and tactics to strengthen the fundamental aspects of your marriage.

This extensive resource offers pragmatic strategies and well-established insights to assist couples in successfully navigating difficulties, reigniting desire, and constructing a durable connection. Now, let's explore the essential tactics that will enable you to actively advocate for and enhance the stability of your marriage.

Effective Communication is Crucial

Transparent and sincere communication is the fundamental basis of a prosperous marital relationship.

The book highlights the significance of good communication, urging couples to communicate their views, feelings, and concerns honestly. Understanding each other's views builds empathy and sets the framework for resolving issues amicably.

Cultivate Emotional Intimacy

Emotional closeness is the glue that holds couples together. The program discusses techniques to renew the emotional connection by stressing quality time, active listening, and vulnerability.

By providing a safe environment for communicating feelings, couples may enhance their knowledge of one another and build the emotional roots of their marriage.

Rediscover Romance and Passion

Over time, the spark of passion may dull, but it may be renewed with purposeful effort.

The guide gives unique ideas and practical ways to bring passion back into your relationship.

From spontaneous gestures to scheduled date nights, finding romance in your marriage leads to a stronger foundation.

Navigating Challenges Together

No marriage is immune to problems, and the book accepts this reality. It prepares couples with effective problem-solving skills, emphasizing the value of cooperation.

Facing hardships together creates resilience, promoting a sense of solidarity and bolstering the foundation against external influences.

Prioritize Self-Care and Individual Growth

Strong marriages are founded on the well-being of each member. The handbook urges couples to emphasize self-care and personal growth. When both couples engage in their individual happiness, it positively benefits the entire health of the marriage, establishing a foundation founded on self-awareness and pleasure.

Establishing Shared Goals and Values

A common vision for the future and related values give a firm basis for a long marriage. The book discusses the process of defining and achieving common goals, generating a feeling of purpose and togetherness. Couples that share objectives and ideals are better suited to weather life's hardships together.

Conclusion

"Rekindle The Love and Discover the Secrets" serves as a manual for couples looking to reinforce the foundations of their marriage. By applying these tactics – from good communication to finding passion and managing problems together – couples may deepen their link and fight for a robust, enduring relationship.

Remember, a firm foundation is the basis upon which a flourishing marriage is created, and with devotion and commitment, you may begin on a road toward a love that withstands the test of time.

THE POWER OF TRUST

Trust is the cornerstone of any good and durable relationship, and in the context of marriage, its value cannot be overemphasized. "Rekindle Love and Discover the Secrets" looks into the transforming power of trust, providing couples practical techniques to not only reestablish trust when it falters but also to proactively cultivate it.

In this examination, we will uncover the tremendous influence of trust on marital dynamics and offer techniques to build this important foundation, allowing couples to fight for their marriage.

Open and Honest Communication

The handbook highlights the crucial significance of open and honest communication in creating and repairing trust.

Couples are urged to create a safe environment for discussion, where they may express themselves without fear of criticism. Transparent communication creates understanding, dismantles misunderstandings, and sets the framework for restoring trust.

Consistency and Reliability

Trust is not only about words but is firmly anchored in deeds.
The handbook highlights the need for consistency and reliability in everyday relationships.
When partners continuously display trustworthiness via their behaviors, it fosters a sense of security and reliability, sustaining the basis of trust within the marriage.

Vulnerability and Empathy

Cultivating trust involves vulnerability and empathy.
The program encourages couples to be open and vulnerable with each other, revealing their worries, hopes, and dreams.
Through empathy, couples may better comprehend each other's viewpoints, building a stronger emotional connection and increasing the trust between them.

Forgiveness and Letting Go

Trust may be tested by mistakes and blunders, but the guide acknowledges the importance of forgiveness in the healing process.
Couples are mentored on the path of letting go of old grievances and embracing forgiveness as a driver for restoring trust.

By accepting shortcomings and learning from mistakes, couples can emerge stronger and more resilient.

46

Do
what
you
love

Setting Limits and Honoring Commitments

Clearly defined limits and honoring commitments is crucial to creating and maintaining trust.

The guide gives insights into the value of mutual respect for personal limits and the relevance of fulfilling promises. Establishing clear expectations helps eliminate misunderstandings and develops an environment of trust and trustworthiness.

Cultivating Trust Through Shared Experiences

Shared experiences generate enduring friendships, and the handbook encourages couples to engage in activities that build trust naturally. Whether it's tackling problems together, attaining joint objectives, or creating shared memories, these experiences develop the basis of trust and contribute to a strong and sustainable marriage.

Conclusion

In the process of rekindling love and understanding the secrets to a happy marriage, trust emerges as a power that connects couples together. "Rekindle Love and Discover the Secrets" offers a guide to harnessing the power of trust, presenting ways that go beyond rebuilding to proactively reinforce this vital factor.

By developing open communication, consistency, vulnerability, forgiveness, and shared experiences, couples may manage the challenges of marriage with a foundation founded on trust.

In the quest for a durable and rewarding relationship, trust becomes the base upon which a strong and everlasting love story is constructed.

CHAPTER TWO

STRENGTHENING YOUR EMOTIONAL BOND

In the delicate dance of marriage, the emotional tie shared between spouses is the pulse of a flourishing partnership.

The "Rekindle Love and Discover the Secrets" guide painstakingly investigates the complexities of emotional connection, giving couples insightful techniques to not only rekindle but also solidify their emotional relationship.

This thorough handbook allows couples to manage the intricacies of marriage with an emphasis on fostering and strengthening the emotional roots of their relationship.

Let's dig into the important methods that will help you on the quest to fight for and develop your marriage emotionally.

Prioritize Quality Time

Quality time is the currency of emotional connection.
The advice underlines the significance of setting out devoted periods for each other despite the rush of daily life.
From personal dinners to shared pastimes, spending quality time develops a stronger emotional link and sustains the connection between partners.

Active Listening and Empathy

Effective communication is a two-way street, and the handbook focuses substantial emphasis on active listening and empathy.
Couples are urged to fully hear and comprehend each other, establishing a sense of emotional validation.
By exercising empathy, couples develop a foundation of support and understanding that deepens their emotional link.

Expressing Vulnerability and Authenticity

The handbook argues for a culture of openness and vulnerability inside the marriage.

Partners are taught to express their true selves, along with concerns, dreams, and doubts. Embracing honesty provides an environment where both persons feel seen and welcomed, enhancing the emotional connection between them.

Cultivate Thanks and Appreciation

Expressing thanks and appreciation is a strong trigger for establishing emotional ties.

The book encourages couples to notice and praise each other's accomplishments, promoting a pleasant and encouraging attitude. Gratitude creates a bridge that links partners on a deeper emotional level.

Navigate Obstacles as a Team

Life's obstacles are unavoidable, but addressing them as a unified front enhances the emotional link between couples.

The book gives techniques for handling obstacles together, emphasizing the value of collaboration.

Overcoming problems cooperatively fosters a sense of trust and unity, deepening the emotional connection.

Celebrate Milestones and Successes

The guide pushes couples to celebrate not just large milestones but also the tiny wins and successes in their path.

Recognizing and remembering triumphs, whether personal or communal, generates a sense of pride and delight, leading to a healthy and emotionally rich marital atmosphere.

Conclusion

"Rekindle Love and Discover the Secrets" stands as a blueprint for couples wishing to deepen their emotional link.

By applying these tactics – from prioritizing quality time and active listening to expressing vulnerability and fostering appreciation – couples may manage the obstacles of marriage with emotional resilience. In the battle for a durable and meaningful relationship, the emotional tie becomes the fabric that weaves together the shared experiences, pleasures, and problems of a successful partnership.

With dedication and intentionality, couples may start on a journey to rediscover and deepen the emotional underpinnings of their love.

THE ART OF ACTIVE LISTENING

In the complicated dance of love and marriage, the capacity to fully listen is a transforming talent that may reinvigorate relationships.

"Rekindle Love and Discover the Secrets" book goes into the skill of active listening, identifying it as a cornerstone for rebuilding the emotional relationships within a marriage.

This thorough guide presents couples with techniques to learn the art of active listening, giving a road to not just handle obstacles but to proactively enhance their relationship.

Let's examine the significant influence of active listening and the solutions it gives to build the foundations of your marriage.

Understanding the Essence of Active Listening

Active listening surpasses just hearing; it requires actively interacting with your partner's words, emotions, and intentions. The tutorial presents the notion of active listening as a dynamic process of being present, absorbing, and reacting with empathy, generating a stronger connection between couples.

Create a Safe and Judgment-Free Place

To foster open conversation, the handbook argues for the construction of a safe and judgment-free place.

Couples are led to develop an environment where both partners feel comfortable expressing their opinions and feelings without fear of condemnation. This secure atmosphere is crucial to good active listening.

Eliminate Distractions

Distractions might inhibit honest conversation.

The book recommends couples remove external distractions when participating in talks. By paying full attention, partners convey the value of the moment and display a dedication to understanding each other, building a stronger emotional connection.

Ask Clarifying Questions

Active listening requires obtaining a comprehensive grasp of your partner's perspective. The tutorial offers the practice of asking clarifying questions to explore deeper into ideas and emotions.

This not only exhibits real attention but also helps to avoid misconceptions that might damage the marital relationship.

Reflective Replies

The handbook highlights the need to deliver reflective replies throughout interactions. Mirroring your partner's feelings and describing their ideas not only improves understanding but also expresses empathy. This reflecting process promotes a sense of affirmation, contributing to the emotional closeness inside the marriage.

Practice Patience and Empathy

Active listening demands patience and empathy.
The guide gives ways to foster these skills, helping couples to calmly listen without interrupting and sympathize with their partner's experiences. This careful and empathic approach creates trust and enhances the emotional fabric of the partnership.

Commit to Continuous Improvement

The art of active listening is a talent that can be cultivated and perfected over time. The approach encourages couples to regard active listening as a continuous commitment to progress. Regularly soliciting feedback from each other and strengthening listening habits develop a culture of continual growth inside the marriage.

Conclusion

Mastering the art of active listening is a great instrument in the armory of marital fortification.

"Rekindle Love and Discover the Secrets" offers as a guide to unraveling the transforming potential of active listening, presenting practical techniques to integrate this ability into the fabric of your relationship.

By providing a safe environment, removing distractions, asking clarifying questions, and practicing patience and empathy, couples may manage problems and proactively improve the emotional roots of their relationship.

In the quest to fight for a lasting and satisfying marriage, the art of active listening becomes a symphony that harmonizes the voices and feelings of both parties, establishing a connection that stands tenacious against the tests of time.

MASTERING CONFLICT RESOLUTION

Conflict is an unavoidable aspect of every relationship; however, the manner in which partners handle and resolve problems can greatly influence the durability and duration of their marriage.

This chapter explores the skill of effectively resolving conflicts, which is a vital component in the process of reigniting love in your marriage.

Analyzing the Essence of Conflict

Conflict emerges due to disparities in viewpoints, principles, and anticipations. Rather than perceiving conflict as indicative of a deteriorating marriage, it can be regarded as a chance for personal development and enhanced comprehension.

This section examines the typical origins of conflict in marital relationships and assists readers in pinpointing the underlying reasons for their arguments.

Optimal Techniques for Effective Communication

Effective communication is essential for resolving conflicts.

This section highlights the significance of transparent, sincere, and courteous communication.

The resource offers practical advice on engaging in active listening, effectively expressing emotions, and employing "I" words to prevent blame and defensiveness.

The Role of Empathy and Understanding

Empathy is a strong tool for settling problems.

Understanding your partner's viewpoint, respecting their feelings, and valuing their experiences helps establish a basis for compromise and resolution.

This section instructs readers on establishing empathy and fostering a stronger relationship through shared understanding.

Conflict Resolution Techniques

Explore a selection of effective dispute-resolution tactics geared toward couples. From compromise and bargaining to finding common ground, this section gives step-by-step tactics for managing issues. Real-life examples and case studies give insights into how these strategies might be utilized in varied marital circumstances.

Time and Place for Resolution

Timing and environment play key roles in effective conflict resolution. This section includes help in finding the correct opportunity to handle disputes, providing a safe environment for talks, and recognizing when to take a brief break to calm off before addressing the topic.

Building Resilience Through Conflict

Resilience is the ability to bounce back from disputes stronger than before. This section addresses how couples may utilize disputes as chances for growth, learning, and deepening their partnership.
It contains exercises and activities to help couples build resilience and protect their relationship against future hardships.

Seeking Professional Guidance

In certain circumstances, disagreements may endure despite efforts to settle them. This section emphasizes the necessity of getting professional help, such as marriage therapy, and gives recommendations on how to approach this choice as a positive step toward marital betterment.

Putting it into Practice

The chapter finishes with practical exercises and concrete actions to help couples execute the dispute resolution tactics outlined. Readers are urged to adopt these tactics in their daily lives, building a better and more harmonious connection.

Mastering conflict resolution is not about avoiding arguments but about managing them in a way that enhances the basis of your marriage. By accepting conflict as a chance for development and learning, couples may reignite the love in their relationship and emerge more connected and resilient than ever before.

IMPORTANCE OF STRENGTHENING YOUR MARRIAGE

The Foundation of a Strong Marriage

A marriage is not only a legal or social commitment; it is a dynamic and changing union between two persons.

At its core, a strong marriage is founded on a foundation of love, trust, and mutual respect. This discusses the essential aspects that contribute to the strength of a marital relationship and highlights the need of creating a firm foundation.

Navigating the Challenges of Marriage

Marriage, like any meaningful partnership, comes with its unique set of obstacles. From communication failures to external stresses, couples regularly confront barriers that might damage their bond. Understanding the main obstacles that couples confront is key in proactively addressing and overcoming them.

The Impact on Individual Well-Being

A healthy marriage favorably promotes the well-being of each spouse individually. Research regularly reveals that persons in happy relationships have improved physical and mental health. This dives into the psychological and physiological benefits of a solid married connection and how investing in your marriage may lead to personal happiness and fulfillment.

Creating a Supportive Environment

A strong marriage creates a supportive atmosphere for personal growth and development.

Couples who feel safe in their relationship are more inclined to pursue their respective goals and dreams.

This analyzes how a supportive marital atmosphere promotes a sense of encouragement, helping each spouse to attain their maximum potential.

The Role in Parenting and Family Dynamics

For couples with children, a solid marriage is the cornerstone of a secure and supportive family environment.

The quality of the marriage connection strongly determines parenting dynamics and, subsequently, the well-being of the entire family unit.

This addresses the relationship between a solid marriage and effective parenting.

Longevity and Resilience

Marriages that endure the test of time feature a level of resilience that comes from conscious attempts to enhance the connection. This discusses the value of longevity in a marriage and how couples may establish a robust link that persists through numerous life phases, struggles, and achievements.

A Source of Emotional Intimacy

Emotional connection is a cornerstone of a happy marriage. Strengthening your marriage strengthens the emotional connection between spouses, generating a greater understanding and regard for each other. This addresses the significance of emotional closeness in marital fulfillment and includes practical recommendations for nurturing this vital part of a good relationship.

Contributing to the Community

A robust and secure marriage benefits favorably to the community at large. Couples that emphasize their connection frequently radiate great energy and act as role models for healthy, successful partnerships. This section examines the larger societal effects of strong marriages and the rippling effect on the community.

Conclusion

The Ongoing Journey of Strengthening Your Marriage

The chapter finishes by highlighting that the road of improving a marriage is ongoing. It involves devotion, communication, and a willingness to adapt and grow together.

As couples put time and effort into reinforcing their relationship, they not only better their individual lives but also contribute to the establishment of a robust and integrated society.

CHAPTER THREE

UNDERSTANDING THE DYNAMICS OF MARRIAGE

Marriage is an intricate and ever-changing voyage that necessitates ongoing exertion, comprehension, and dedication from both individuals involved. As time passes, the first feeling of intense love may diminish, and difficulties might emerge.

Nevertheless, by actively striving to comprehend the intricacies of matrimony, couples may not only successfully navigate through challenging periods but also reignite the passion and affection in their relationship. This will explore the fundamental elements of comprehending the mechanics of marriage and revitalizing the affection that first united two persons.

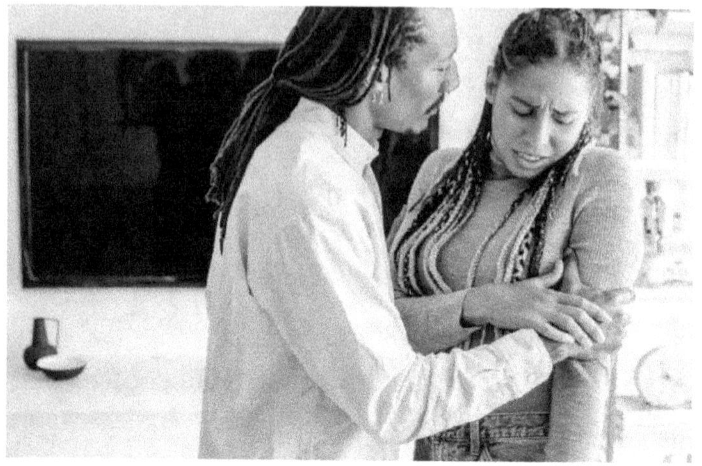

Effective Communication is Crucial

The cornerstone of a thriving marital relationship is on transparent and sincere communication.

It is important for couples to communicate their emotions, requirements, and worries in an efficient manner.

Devote sufficient time to engage in active listening to your spouse and make a conscious effort to comprehend their viewpoint. Effective communication promotes the development of intimacy, trust, and emotional bonding.

Emotional Intimacy

Emotional intimacy entails establishing a profound connection at an emotional level. Share your ideas, worries, and dreams with your companion. Create a safe space for vulnerability and urge your partner to do the same.

The greater the emotional connection, the more resilient the marriage becomes.

Quality Time Together

Amidst the rush and bustle of daily life, it's vital to carve out meaningful time for each other. Engage in things that you both love, whether it's a date night, a weekend vacation, or simply spending peaceful time together. Quality time enhances the link between partners.

Understanding and Empathy

Each member contributes their unique experiences, viewpoints, and emotions into a marriage.

Understanding and empathy are key in negotiating differences.

Take the time to grasp your partner's point of view, and build an environment of mutual respect and support.

Managing Conflicts

Conflicts are unavoidable in any relationship, but how they are managed is crucial. Learn constructive conflict resolution techniques, such as active listening, compromise, and finding common ground. Addressing conflicts with respect and empathy may lead to resolution and progress.

Rediscovering Romance

Rekindling love frequently entails rediscovering the romantic parts of your relationship. Surprise your sweetheart with gestures that remind them of your early days together.

This might be penning love letters, arranging impromptu events, or just expressing gratitude for each other.

Individual Growth and Support

Marriage includes the progress of both persons. Encourage each other's personal growth and encourage individual aspirations. Celebrate triumphs and face obstacles together.

A great partnership is based on the basis of two thriving individuals.

Intimacy and Physical Connection

Physical closeness is a fundamental component of a love relationship. Pay attention to the physical parts of your relationship, ensuring that both parties feel wanted and pleased.

Experiment with strategies to increase your physical connection and keep the desire alive.

Conclusion

Understanding the dynamics of marriage is an ongoing process that demands devotion and effort from both spouses.

By cultivating efficient communication, emotional closeness, quality time, understanding, and support, couples may manage problems and reignite the love that brought them together.

It's an investment in a flourishing, lasting marriage that withstands the test of time.

THE RULES OF ENGAGEMENT

Rekindling the flame in a relationship demands a purposeful and thorough approach. The rules of engagement in reigniting love are fundamental recommendations that couples can follow to traverse the road of rediscovery. In this thorough book, we will discuss the fundamental ideas and acts that contribute to effectively rekindling love in a relationship.

Open Communication

The core of every effective rekindling endeavor is open and honest communication. Partners should share their thoughts, aspirations, and concerns without fear of condemnation. Establishing a secure place for free communication improves understanding and lays the way for a deeper emotional connection.

Reflective Listening

Beyond just stating one's thoughts, engaged in mindful listening is vital. Take the time to genuinely hear and grasp your partner's perspective. This method builds empathy and guarantees that both persons feel noticed and respected.

Acknowledging Issues

To reignite love, couples must address underlying issues that may have contributed to a downturn in the relationship.

This involves a willingness to accept and work through obstacles, embracing vulnerability and humility in the process.

Setting Realistic Expectations

Unrealistic expectations can damage a relationship.

Set reasonable objectives for the rekindling process, realizing that it is a journey with its ups and downs.

Patience and a realistic outlook will help both parties manage expectations and avoid unneeded disappointment.

Quality Time and Shared Experiences

Actively invest time in each other.

Plan activities that generate delight and build shared memories.

These shared experiences deepen the tie between spouses, promoting a sense of connection and oneness.

Reignite Romance

Rekindling love frequently entails a renewal of romanticism. Partners should make a conscious effort to bring back elements of romance into their relationship.

Surprise gestures, thoughtful presents, and demonstrations of affection can renew the spark that first attracted them together.

94

Forgiveness and Letting Go

Forgiveness is a significant instrument in the rekindling process. Both spouses must be willing to forgive previous errors and let go of residual resentments. This offers space for a fresh start and allows the relationship to flourish healthily.

Spontaneity and Variety

Injecting surprise and variation into the relationship helps break the routine and restore enthusiasm.

Explore new activities together, explore new hobbies, or embark on adventures. Novelty and variation excite the relationship, keeping it from becoming stale.

Intimacy and Physical Connection

Physical contact is a fundamental part of rekindling love. Partners should focus the physical connection through affection, contact, and intimacy.

It increases the emotional tie and reignites the desire between them.

Celebrate Progress

Celebrate the minor successes and progress accomplished throughout the rekindling process.

Recognizing and recognizing good developments motivates both partners to stay engaged to the process and develops a sense of success.

Conclusion

Rekindling love is a shared process that involves dedication, patience, and a willingness to welcome change.

By following to the norms of engagement, couples may traverse the path of rediscovery with purpose and develop a revitalized and deepened relationship that endures the test of time.

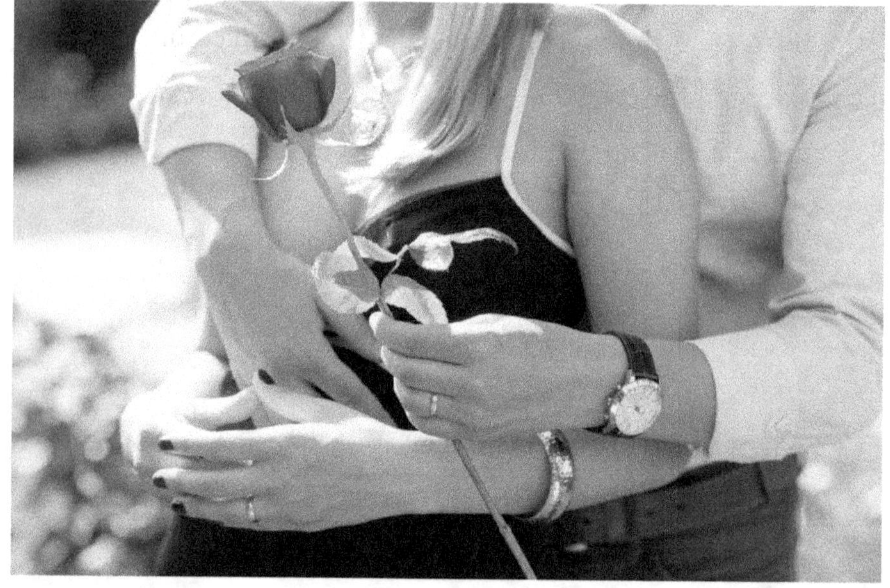

FOUNDATION OF A STRONG MARRIAGE

A strong and enduring marriage is founded on a foundation of love, trust, and mutual respect. As couples travel the road of marriage, obstacles are inevitable, but it's the dedication to rekindling love that truly fortifies the bond. In this investigation of "Rekindle The Love," we look into the basic factors that create the cornerstone of a solid and sustainable marital relationship.

Communication is Key

Effective communication is the cornerstone of any successful marriage. Open and honest discussion creates understanding, empathy, and a sense of connection between couples.

"Rekindle The Love" highlights the necessity of carefully listening to each other's thoughts and feelings, establishing a safe environment for expression, and addressing concerns constructively. Couples who communicate well are better suited to manage obstacles and grow together.

Trust and Transparency

Trust is the glue that ties a marriage together. Building and retaining trust needs openness and consistency.

"Rekindle The Love" urges couples to be open about their ideas, emotions, and problems. By building a trusting atmosphere, partners can rely on each other, which strengthens the emotional stability of the partnership.

Shared Values and Objectives

A good marriage is founded in shared values and mutual objectives. "Rekindle The Love" underlines the necessity of harmonizing underlying ideas and objectives. Couples that have a vision for their future are more likely to overcome hurdles, work together, and find fulfillment in their path together.

Quality Time and Intimacy

Nurturing the romantic and intimate sides of a relationship is vital. Spending quality time together, whether via similar activities, date evenings, or simple moments of connection, helps keep the flame alive. "Rekindle The Love" highlights the value of physical and emotional closeness, encouraging a deeper link between lovers.

Resilience and Adaptation

Life is full of unexpected twists and turns, and a good marriage demands resilience and adaptation. "Rekindle The Love" urges couples to tackle obstacles as a team, learning and developing together through hardship. The capacity to adapt to changing circumstances and support each other during trying times improves the marital foundation.

Ongoing Growth and Learning

A happy marriage is a journey of ongoing growth and learning. "Rekindle The Love" promotes for personal development and mutual support in the achievement of individual and common goals. Couples who engage in their individual growth contribute to the overall health and vibrancy of the relationship.

Conclusion

"Rekindle The Love" underlines the necessity of conscious work, communication, and dedication in developing a healthy marriage foundation. By prioritizing love, trust, shared values, closeness, resilience, and ongoing growth, couples may not only overcome obstacles but also form a long and satisfying partnership.

In the journey of marriage, the foundation is not just set once; it takes ongoing care and attention to guarantee it remains strong and durable throughout the years.

COMMON CHALLENGES FACED IN MARRIAGE

Marriage is a great experience, but it comes with its fair share of obstacles. Couples regularly confront many hurdles that might strain their relationship, leading to misunderstandings, communication breakdowns, and emotional distance.

In this book, we discuss common issues faced in marriage and present techniques to rekindle the love, establishing a strong and enduring commitment.

Communication Breakdown

One of the most typical issues in marriage is communication breakdown. Couples often struggle to articulate their needs and feelings properly, resulting to misunderstandings and resentment. To overcome this challenge, it is vital to create open and honest communication.

Regular check-ins, active listening, and expressing emotions in a healthy manner can pave the path for a closer connection.

Emotional Distance

Over time, couples may find themselves growing emotionally distant. This can be a result of hectic schedules, stress, or unresolved difficulties. To reignite the emotional spark, it is crucial to focus quality time together.

Date nights, common activities, and honest conversations about feelings can help bridge the emotional divide, building connection and understanding.

Closeness Issues

Physical closeness plays a significant role in a healthy marriage. However, numerous causes such as stress, weariness, and changing priorities might contribute to intimacy troubles.

Couples need to prioritize and devote time in preserving their physical connection. Exploring each other's passions, being attentive to each other's needs, and keeping the romance alive are vital components in rekindling intimacy.

Financial Strain

Financial issues can put a strain on any relationship. Divergent spending habits, clashing financial goals, or unanticipated expenses might create tension.

Developing a clear financial plan, setting mutual financial goals, and promoting open conversation about money helps ease financial stress and strengthen the basis of the marriage.

Conflicting Priorities

As life evolves, individual goals and priorities may alter, leading to disputes within the marriage. It's crucial for couples to regularly examine and align their goals.

Finding common ground, compromise, and supporting each other's aspirations are vital for maintaining a harmonious and supportive partnership.

STRATEGIES FOR STRENGTHENING YOUR MARRIAGE

Prioritize Communication

Make communication a priority by setting aside dedicated time for open and honest interactions. Regularly check in with each other about your feelings, worries, and objectives.

Invest in Quality Time

Allocate quality time for shared activities and experiences. Whether it's a weekly date night, a weekend getaway, or simply spending nights together, developing meaningful connections outside regular routines is crucial.

Seek Professional Help

If troubles persist, seeking the help of a marriage counselor can provide essential insights and techniques for navigating complex issues. Professional support can help couples understand each other better and establish solutions for overcoming obstacles.

Welcome Change Together

As individuals and as a marriage, welcome personal and collective progress. Be willing to adapt to change and support one other's progress, generating a sense of togetherness and shared purpose.

In conclusion, marriage involves ongoing work, understanding, and adaptation.

By addressing common issues through good communication, emphasizing intimacy, and accepting change together, couples can not only overcome obstacles but also develop a durable and robust partnership. Rekindling the love in a marriage involves a dedication to each other's well-being and a shared path toward a stronger, more rewarding union.

BREAKING DOWN BARRIERS

Marriage is a precious bond that often meets barriers that can threaten its basis. The journey of a married marriage is filled with ups and downs, and conquering challenges requires effort, understanding, and effective solutions.

In this book, we look into the common difficulties experienced in marriage and share ideas on how to reignite the love, along with secret tactics to strengthen your marriage.

Communication Challenges

Effective communication is the cornerstone of a healthy marriage. Yet, couples often experience difficulty in communicating their views and feelings.

To break down communication barriers, it's vital to cultivate active listening skills and provide a secure setting for open discourse.

Regularly check in with your partner, expressing concerns and happiness, establishing a deeper relationship.

Emotional Disconnect

Over time, couples may find themselves emotionally distant owing to several circumstances, including stress, routine, or unresolved concerns. To rekindle the emotional spark, prioritize emotional closeness. Share your vulnerabilities, engage in activities that build emotional connection, and make efforts to comprehend your partner's feelings.

Trust Issues

Trust forms the bedrock of a good marriage, but it can be damaged by breaches of confidence or past grievances.
 Rebuilding trust needs transparency, responsibility, and constant effort. Establishing open discussion regarding trust concerns, finding understanding, and working together to reestablish trust helps enhance the marital bond.

Intimacy Struggles

 Physical intimacy is a key element of marriage, but numerous challenges such as stress, weariness, or monotony can contribute to intimacy struggles. Break down these walls by prioritizing intimate times, exploring each other's desires, and retaining a sense of spontaneity. Reviving passion and closeness can reignite the spark in your marriage.

External Pressures

External pressures, such as work commitments, family expectations, or society influences, can strain a marriage. To overcome these difficulties, couples must create boundaries, prioritize their relationship, and work together to navigate external influences. Developing a united front against external obstacles helps enhance the marriage.

STRATEGIES FOR STRENGTHENING YOUR MARRIAGE

Practice Active Listening

Listen intently to your partner's worries, feelings, and objectives. Create an environment where both partners feel heard and understood, encouraging a deeper relationship.

Schedule Quality Time

Set aside allocated time for meaningful conversations.
Whether it's a weekly date night or a weekend getaway, prioritize quality time to strengthen your connection and break away from routine.

Cultivate Emotional Intimacy

Share your emotions and encourage your spouse to do the same. Cultivating emotional closeness includes creating a safe space for vulnerability, empathy, and understanding.

Rebuild Trust Through Transparency

If trust has been eroded, aim towards repairing it through transparency and accountability. Openly discuss concerns, create boundaries, and display consistent trustworthy conduct.

Prioritize Your Relationship

Amidst life's hardships, prioritize your marriage.

Set boundaries with external demands, make mutual decisions, and actively work together to protect and improve your partnership.

In conclusion, breaking down barriers in a marriage needs proactive efforts, excellent communication, and a commitment to mutual improvement.

By applying these tactics, couples can reignite the love, learn the keys to a lasting union, and fortify their marriage against the hardships that emerge.

Fighting for your marriage takes a joint commitment to overcome hurdles, creating a deep connection, and building a robust foundation for a lifetime of love.

STRATEGIES TO OVERCOME BARRIERS

Marriage, while a source of joy and companionship, often faces challenges that can strain the relationship.

Overcoming these barriers requires a combination of commitment, communication, and intentional effort.

In this guide, we explore effective strategies to rekindle the love, unravel the secrets to a strong marriage, and provide insights on how to fight for and strengthen your lifelong partnership.

Open and Honest Communication

One of the fundamental pillars of a successful marriage is communication. Barriers often arise when couples fail to express their needs, concerns, and feelings.

To overcome this, prioritize open and honest communication. Create a safe space where both partners feel comfortable sharing their thoughts and emotions without fear of judgment.

Regular check-ins and active listening foster understanding, laying the groundwork for a resilient connection.

Cultivate Emotional Intimacy

Emotional intimacy is the glue that binds couples together. However, daily demands and routine can erode this intimacy. To reignite the emotional spark, cultivate shared experiences, and create opportunities for vulnerability. Expressing emotions, sharing dreams, and being present for each other in both good and challenging times deepen the emotional connection, strengthening the marital bond.

Address Trust Issues

Trust is a delicate aspect of any relationship, and its erosion can create significant barriers. To rebuild trust, couples must address the root causes of the issues, engage in open dialogue, and commit to transparency. Rebuilding trust takes time and consistent effort, but it is essential for fostering a secure foundation in the marriage.

Prioritize Quality Time

In the hustle and bustle of daily life, couples often find themselves overwhelmed with responsibilities, leaving little time for each other. To overcome this barrier, prioritize quality time together. Schedule regular date nights, weekend getaways, or even simple moments of connection. Investing time in shared experiences helps build lasting memories and strengthens the bond between partners.

Tackle Intimacy Struggles

Physical intimacy is a crucial component of a thriving marriage, yet various factors can create barriers.

To address intimacy struggles, initiate open conversations about desires, preferences, and concerns.

Create an atmosphere of comfort and trust, allowing both partners to express their needs and work together to rekindle the passion in their physical connection.

STRATEGIES FOR STRENGTHENING YOUR MARRIAGE

Continuous Learning

Couples who invest in learning together often find new ways to connect. Attend workshops, read books, or engage in activities that promote personal and relational growth. Learning together not only strengthens your bond but also provides fresh perspectives on common challenges.

Seek Professional Help

When barriers seem insurmountable, seeking the assistance of a marriage counselor can provide valuable insights.
Professional guidance helps couples navigate complex issues, facilitating better communication and understanding.

Practice Gratitude

Expressing gratitude for your partner and the positive aspects of your relationship can transform your perspective.

Regularly acknowledging and appreciating each other fosters a positive atmosphere, making it easier to overcome challenges.

Embrace Flexibility

Marriage is a dynamic journey that requires adaptability.

Embrace flexibility in your expectations and be open to compromise. A willingness to adjust and grow together promotes a resilient and enduring partnership.

In conclusion, strategies to overcome barriers in a marriage involve a combination of effective communication, emotional intimacy, trust-building, and intentional efforts to prioritize the relationship. By implementing these strategies and remaining committed to the journey of growth together, couples can not only rekindle the love but also discover the secrets to a lasting and fulfilling marriage. Fighting for your marriage involves active participation, mutual understanding, and a shared commitment to building a resilient foundation for a lifetime of love and companionship.

REIGNITING THE SPARK IN YOUR MARRIAGE

Marriage, like any other journey, can have lulls where the original spark fades. Couples can reignite the flame and find the joy in their relationship with intention, effort, and the correct tactics.

In this book, we will look at successful tactics for rekindling love and uncovering the keys to a stronger marriage, as well as how to actively fight for and maintain your lasting commitment.

Make Quality Time a Priority

Couples frequently drift away in the middle of daily activities. Prioritize quality time together to rekindle the flame.

Whether it's a romantic dinner, a weekend getaway, or a peaceful evening at home, spending time with each other promotes connection and intimacy.

Couples can rediscover shared interests, make new experiences, and enhance their emotional tie by spending quality time together.

Communicate Desires Openly

Individual interests and needs change as partnerships change.

It is critical to have open communication regarding these changing desires. Make a comfortable environment for open discussions about personal and shared goals, desires, and fantasies. Recognizing and understanding each other's desires can lead to a renewed sense of closeness and connection.

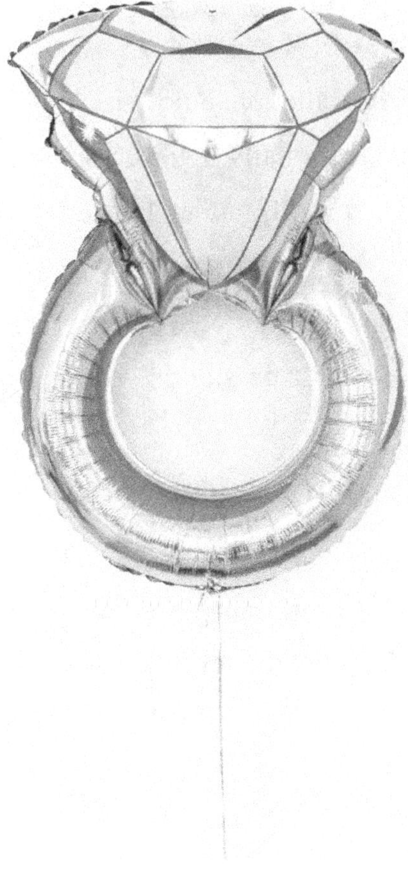

Rediscover Common Interests

Couples are frequently caught up in routine, forgetting shared pastimes that formerly provided them joy.

Rediscover these activities to rekindle the flame.

Whether it's a long-forgotten hobby or a new passion, sharing common interests creates friendship and adds new life to the relationship.

Develop Emotional Intimacy

A strong marriage is built on emotional closeness.

Take the time to connect emotionally by discussing your feelings, anxieties, and goals. Make yourself vulnerable and encourage your partner to do the same.

Creating a safe environment for emotional intimacy strengthens your bond and helps to revive the passion in your relationship.

Take turns Surprising each other

Surprises, big or small, can add excitement to a marriage.

To keep the flame alive, plan surprising gestures, presents, or romantic outings. Surprises show thoughtfulness and an ongoing commitment to making your partner feel valued and cherished.

MARRIAGE STRENGTHENING STRATEGIES

Renewal of Vows

Consider renewing your wedding vows as a symbolic act of love and commitment. This ceremony can serve as a strong reminder of why you selected one other in the first place, as well as rekindle your sense of togetherness and commitment to your marriage.

Participate in Relationship Workshops or Counseling

Attending relationship courses or getting professional counseling can provide useful tools and insights.

These services provide a controlled atmosphere for couples to resolve concerns, improve communication, and get a better knowledge of one another.

Develop Gratitude

Gratitude for your partner and the positive parts of your relationship might help you change your emphasis from issues to blessings. Recognizing and appreciating one another on a regular basis deepens the foundation of love and connection.

144

Establish New Shared Objectives

Set new goals as a pair, whether they are for personal development, travel, or shared experiences.

Working toward shared goals promotes a sense of partnership and teamwork, reigniting the fire in your path together.

To summarize, reigniting the flame in your marriage needs deliberate work, open communication, and a commitment to shared progress. Couples can recapture the love that brought them together by emphasizing quality time, developing emotional closeness, and introducing surprises into their relationship. Fighting for your marriage is actively pursuing techniques that keep the flame alive, ensuring a durable and fulfilling union for years to come.

CHAPTER FOUR
COMMUNICATION STRATEGIES

In the complicated dance of marriage, efficient communication serves as the linchpin that either forges stronger ties or creates barriers. The process of rekindling love and uncovering the secrets of rebuilding a marriage is delicately braided with communication tactics that go beyond words. In this thorough guide, we disclose important communication tactics that can breathe new life into your relationship, delivering ideas on how to fight for and build the foundation of your marriage.

Active Listening as a Foundation

Rekindling love begins with active listening.

In the hurry of daily life, partners frequently overlook the power of actually hearing each other.

Make a conscious effort to listen without judging, interrupting, or crafting a response as your spouse speaks.

Actively listening creates a safe space for vulnerability, developing understanding and closeness.

Expressing Vulnerability

The secret to strengthening a marriage rests in displaying vulnerability. Share your concerns, dreams, and insecurities with your companion. This transparency builds a profound relationship and establishes a foundation of trust.

Vulnerability is a gateway to mutual understanding, allowing partners to see one other in their most real light.

Non-Verbal Communication

While words are vital, non-verbal cues play a significant part in communication. A delicate touch, a comforting glance, or a warm smile can transmit feelings more powerfully than words alone.

Pay attention to these non-verbal signs and use them carefully to show love, understanding, and support.

Timing and Tone

Understanding the importance of timing and tone is vital in marital communication. Avoid discussing delicate things in the heat of the moment. Instead, find a time when both parties are calm and receptive. The tone of communication establishes the emotional tone of the discourse, therefore strive for a courteous and empathic approach.

The Art of Compromise

Successful communication in marriage entails the art of compromise. Recognize that differences are natural and welcome the opportunity to establish common ground.

In compromise, both partners contribute to the progress of the relationship, generating a sense of togetherness and cooperation.

Using "I" Statements

When expressing demands, concerns, or desires, structure your words using "I" rather than "you." For example, use "I feel unheard when…" instead of "You never listen."

This redirects the focus to your feelings and experiences, eliminating defensiveness and enabling a more meaningful discourse.

Regular Check-Ins

Frequent communication check-ins serve as a proactive measure to comprehend each other's growing needs and moods.

Make these check-ins a frequent part of your routine, ensuring that both partners feel heard and respected.

This continual discourse cultivates a culture of openness and responsiveness in the marriage.

Building Emotional Resilience

Marriage is not immune to hardships, and creating emotional resilience via communication is vital.

Acknowledge that issues may come, and when they do, address them together. Discussing difficulties openly, without blame or criticism, enhances the emotional resilience of the relationship.

Shared Goal Setting

Communication gains purpose when it coincides with common goals. Work together to develop short-term and long-term goals for your marriage. This joint effort generates a sense of cooperation, generating a shared vision that enhances the link between partners.

Seeking Professional Guidance

When communication hurdles remain, seeking the guidance of a professional can be trans formative.

Marriage counselors provide a neutral environment for couples to explore challenging issues, offering skills and insights to promote communication and understanding.

In conclusion, communication tactics are the lifeblood of a thriving marriage. Rekindling love, unearthing secrets, and battling for your marriage all rest on the ability of efficient communication.

By adopting these tactics throughout your regular interactions, you not only improve your connection but also develop a sturdy basis for a durable and fulfilling partnership. In the arena of marriage, communication is not just a talent; it is the heart and soul of love's enduring journey.

EFFECTIVE COMMUNICATION SKILLS AND OVERCOMING COMMUNICATION BARRIERS

Communication is the heartbeat of a good and thriving marriage. It serves as the gateway for knowledge, closeness, and connection. In the process of rekindling love and uncovering the secrets to a lasting partnership, excellent communication skills play a pivotal role. This thorough guide addresses not only the fundamental components of communication but also provides effective techniques to overcome typical hurdles, helping couples to enhance their bond and negotiate the difficulties of marriage.

THE FOUNDATION OF EFFECTIVE COMMUNICATION

Active Listening

At the heart of effective communication is attentive listening. This skill goes beyond only hearing words; it entails thoroughly understanding the emotions, motivations, and views behind the communication. In the context of marriage, active listening fosters an environment where partners feel truly heard and respected. Practice this skill by giving your partner entire attention, restraining judgment, and responding empathetically. Active listening creates the foundation for meaningful and constructive conversations.

Clear and Concise Expression

Communication is most impactful when it is clear and straightforward. The capacity to explain thoughts and feelings in a simple manner avoids misconceptions and facilitates efficient communication. Couples can work on this skill by communicating their opinions with clearly, avoiding superfluous jargon, and ensuring that their message is easily received.

Clear expression encourages honesty and authenticity in marital communication.

Empathy in Communication

Empathy is the bridge that unites couples on a deeper emotional level. It entails knowing and sharing the feelings of the other person. In the context of marriage, exercising empathy includes understanding and validating each other's emotions.

This creates a safe space for vulnerability and builds a profound connection. Empathy is not simply about comprehending; it is about exhibiting that understanding through words and deeds.

Non-Verbal Communication

Beyond words, non-verbal cues play a key part in communication. Facial expressions, body language, and tone of voice convey feelings that words alone may not describe.

Couples can strengthen their non-verbal communication by being attentive of these indicators and aligning them with spoken expressions. A touch, a smile, or a compassionate stare can communicate love, support, and understanding more powerfully than words.

Choose the Right Medium

The medium of communication can considerably impact its effectiveness. In today's digitally driven world, couples may interact through different channels, including face-to-face discussions, phone calls, or text messaging.

Understanding the context and aim of the communication assists in selecting the most appropriate media.

Certain messages are best given in person, while others may be more ideal for written communication.

Feedback Loop

Establishing a feedback loop is vital for strengthening communication abilities. Encouraging open discussion regarding communication itself gives a space for partners to provide constructive feedback. This two-way interaction encourages continual progress, ensuring that both participants feel heard and understood. A healthy feedback loop increases the communication dynamics inside a marriage.

OVERCOMING COMMUNICATION BARRIERS

Timing and Tone

Two key factors of effective communication are timing and tone. Choosing the correct time to launch critical talks is vital.

 Avoid discussing delicate things in the heat of the moment and wait for a time when both partners are calm and attentive.

The tone of communication sets the emotional tone of the interaction. Strive for a courteous and empathic attitude, ensuring that the message is received in the intended spirit.

The Art of Compromise

Conflict is inherent in any relationship, but excellent communication may transform disputes into chances for growth.

The art of compromise requires acknowledging that differences are natural and seeking common ground.

Both spouses participate to the resolution of disagreements, generating a sense of unity and cooperation.

Communicate your demands and viewpoints, but also be open to understanding your partner's point of view.

Using "I" Statements

The language used in communication can either inspire collaboration or lead to defensiveness. Using "I" statements instead of "you" statements shifts the focus on personal sentiments and experiences. For example, saying, "I feel unheard when..." is less accusatory than saying, "You never listen."
This slight shift facilitates a more constructive and empathic discourse, lowering the possibility of defensive responses.

Regular Check-Ins

Proactive communication entails regular check-ins to comprehend each other's shifting needs and sentiments.

Make these check-ins a routine aspect of your partnership. Creating a space for open and honest discussion ensures that both partners feel heard and respected.

Regular communication check-ins promote a culture of responsiveness and prevent issues from worsening.

Building Emotional Resilience

Emotional resilience is a critical part in overcoming communication hurdles.

Acknowledge that obstacles will emerge, and when they do, address them together.

Discuss concerns freely, concentrating on the matter at hand rather than engaging in personal attacks.

Building emotional resilience through effective communication allows couples to navigate hardships while strengthening the foundation of their relationship.

Shared Goal Setting

Effective communication gains purpose when it connects with common goals. Work together to develop short-term and long-term goals for your marriage.

Collaborative goal setting develops a sense of teamwork, producing a shared vision that enhances the link between partners. Aligning communication with common objectives adds direction and meaning to your interactions.

Seeking Professional Guidance

When communication hurdles remain, seeking the guidance of a professional can be transformative.

Marriage counselors offer neutral ground for couples to negotiate challenging issues. Professional guidance gives skills and insights that promote communication and comprehension.

Overcoming communication hurdles with the help of a counselor can breathe new life into a marriage and offer a fresh perspective on persistent concerns.

Conclusion

In the complicated dance of marriage, excellent communication skills are the threads that weave the fabric of connection and understanding. Rekindling love and understanding the secrets to a lasting partnership need a dedication to honing these talents and overcoming communication barriers.

By carefully listening, displaying vulnerability, practicing empathy, and learning the nuances of non-verbal communication, partners can build a deep and meaningful relationship.

Moreover, overcoming communication hurdles includes managing the subtleties of timing and tone, embracing the art of compromise, and utilizing language that invites collaboration.

Regular check-ins, collaborative goal planning, and cultivating emotional resilience establish a sturdy foundation for a marriage that can weather the test of time.

Ultimately, receiving professional help when needed is a testimonial to the commitment to growth and understanding within a marriage. Effective communication is not a one-time accomplishment but a continuing process of refinement and progress.

In the process of rekindling love and uncovering the keys to a successful partnership, mastering the art of connection through excellent communication skills is the key to a thriving and fulfilling marriage.

DEALING AND COPING WITH EXTERNAL PRESSURES

In the complicated dance of marriage, external influences often take center stage, testing the strength of the tie between partners. However, the secret to a durable and fulfilling marriage lies in the ability to negotiate and overcome these external problems.

In this book guide, we will delve into useful tactics and secrets to not only manage with external stresses but also rekindle the love that initially drew you together.

Let's go on a journey to improve the foundation of your marriage and learn how to fight for the love you both deserve.

Understanding External Pressures

Marriage is a delicate blend of shared joys and hardships.

External pressures can occur in different forms, such as financial strain, work-related stress, family issues, and societal expectations. Recognizing and understanding these challenges is the first step toward addressing them effectively.

It's vital to tackle external obstacles as a united front, knowing that both spouses play a role in conquering them.

Communication The Cornerstone of a Strong Marriage

Effective communication is the cornerstone of any successful marriage. When faced with external demands, open and honest communication becomes even more crucial.

Create a secure atmosphere where both partners feel comfortable expressing their thoughts and emotions without fear of criticism. Regular check-ins, sincere conversations, and attentive listening are great strategies to reinforce your relationship and understanding.

Setting Realistic Expectations

One typical source of external strain in marriages is the unreasonable expectations we impose on ourselves and our partners. It's necessary to create realistic expectations regarding duties, obligations, and the trajectory of the relationship.

Discuss your goals, aspirations, and potential challenges honestly, ensuring that both parties are on the same page.

Adjusting expectations to coincide with reality can dramatically reduce stress and strengthen your marriage.

Financial Harmony

Financial strain is a prominent cause of external pressure in marriages. It's vital to develop open discussion about money matters and work together to set a realistic budget.

Consider creating financial goals as a partnership and finding compromises that match with both partners' values.

Building a stable financial foundation can ease stress and allow you to focus on strengthening your relationship.

Quality Time and Intimacy

Amidst external pressures, couples sometimes find themselves neglecting the basic cornerstone of their connection—quality time and intimacy. Schedule frequent date nights, weekend trips, or simply simple moments of connection amidst your busy lives. Rekindling the spark involves purposeful effort, and prioritizing quality time together is an effective technique to enhance your bond.

Counseling and Support

Sometimes, external demands may become overbearing, and seeking professional help can be a transforming step.

Marriage counseling provides a secure space for couples to address their concerns, uncover deeper issues, and learn effective coping skills.

Additionally, seeking support from friends, family, or support groups can offer vital views and encouragement during hard times.

174

Embracing Change and Adaptability

Life is dynamic, and external forces are unavoidable. Embracing change and building adaptability are crucial for a happy marriage. Instead of opposing problems, view them as chances for growth and transformation.

Develop an attitude that helps you to tackle adversity together, emerging stronger as a partnership.

Cultivating Individual and Collective Growth

A strong marriage is based on the foundation of individual and collective progress. Encourage each other's personal development, encouraging objectives and dreams.

As individuals grow, so does the strength of the partnership. Celebrate victories, no matter how minor, and face problems as a single front, establishing a sense of mutual accomplishment.

Rekindling Romance and Rediscovering Love

To fight for your marriage, it's vital to rekindle the passion and rediscover the love that brought you together.

Nurture the emotional and physical parts of your relationship through gestures of love, surprise acts of kindness, and shared experiences. Rediscovering the delight of being with each other can reignite the flame and create a sturdy foundation for your marriage.

Conclusion

In the journey of marriage, external forces are inevitable, but they don't have to define the trajectory of your partnership.

By applying the tactics given in this guide, you can not only manage with external stresses but also enhance your marriage and rediscover the love that initially drew you together.

Remember, a strong marriage involves ongoing work, honest communication, and a mutual commitment to endure the storms together. Embrace the adventure, fight for your love, and develop a sturdy foundation that will weather the tests of time.

BALANCING CAREER AND MARRIAGE

In the fast-paced and demanding world we live in, the delicate dance between career and marriage frequently becomes a tough balancing act. Juggling professional aspirations with the obligations of a committed relationship may be daunting, leading many couples to feel alienated and strained.

However, there is hope. This thorough guide is aimed to offer practical techniques to reignite the love in your marriage while handling the pressures of a prosperous profession.

Understanding the Dynamics

To begin the road of rekindling love, it's vital to grasp the dynamics at play. Recognize that both spouses contribute unique assets and challenges to the partnership.

A successful marriage includes accepting and appreciating these differences while retaining a shared vision for the future.

Explore your individual job ambitions and how they match with your collective aspirations as a couple.

EFFECTIVE COMMUNICATION

Communication is the cornerstone of any successful relationship. Develop open and honest avenues of communication with your partner. Schedule regular check-ins to discuss both personal and professional elements of your lives.

Actively listen to your partner's concerns and objectives, and express yours in return.

By building an environment of trust and understanding, you lay the foundation for a durable and loving relationship.

Prioritizing Quality Time

In the middle of busy schedules and work pressures, it's crucial to carve out quality time for your relationship.

Whether it's a weekly date night, a weekend getaway, or simply spending uninterrupted time together at home, prioritize moments that enhance your emotional connection.

Quality time deepens the relationship between spouses and acts as a reminder of the love that brought you together in the first place.

Balancing Career Demands

Successfully managing job and marriage needs efficient time management. Set realistic expectations for work hours and commitments, ensuring that both couples contribute to creating a balanced lifestyle. It may include establishing boundaries with your workplace, learning to delegate chores, or even reevaluating career ambitions to coincide with the needs of your relationship.

Shared Goals and Dreams

Discovering shared objectives and dreams is crucial to creating a good foundation for your marriage.

While individual job objectives are vital, identifying common aims offers a sense of unity and purpose.

Work together to set short-term and long-term goals that accommodate both professional and personal desires, generating a spirit of collaboration and mutual support.

Intimacy and Romance

Nurturing intimacy is crucial for rekindling love in a marriage. Make a conscious effort to keep the romance alive by engaging in activities that encourage emotional and physical closeness.

Surprise your partner with meaningful gestures, show appreciation for each other, and value times of connection.

A successful private life adds greatly to the overall health and happiness of your partnership.

Seeking Professional Guidance

Sometimes, despite our best efforts, issues may occur that necessitate expert involvement.

Consider seeking the help of a marriage counselor or therapist.

Professional guidance can offer essential insights, communication techniques, and coping strategies to handle the complications of managing profession and marriage.

 It's a proactive step that indicates devotion to the relationship's well-being.

Growing Together

Marriage is a journey of progress, both individually and as a pair. Embrace change and adaptability, knowing that personal and professional development are continual processes.

Celebrate each other's triumphs and encourage one another through obstacles. By growing together, you build the foundation of your marriage and create a sturdy union capable of withstanding the strains of time.

A Lifelong Commitment to Love

Balancing career and marriage is a constant journey that takes focus, communication, and a shared commitment to love.

By applying these tactics, couples can rekindle the flame of their relationship, strengthen their relationships, and manage the complexity of modern life together.

Remember, the journey of a successful marriage is a team endeavor, where both couples actively contribute to create a satisfying and peaceful existence together.

Building and Maintaining Emotional Intimacy

In the complicated tapestry of marriage, emotional intimacy acts as the key thread that links partners together.

In the midst of life's obstacles, preserving and expanding upon this emotional connection becomes important for a durable and successful partnership.

This comprehensive guide discusses techniques to reignite the love in your marriage by emphasizing the importance of emotional connection and provides specific steps to build this cornerstone.

Understanding Emotional Intimacy

Before delving into techniques, it's vital to grasp what emotional closeness genuinely entails.

Emotional intimacy means communicating your deepest thoughts, worries, and desires with your spouse.

It's about developing a climate of trust, vulnerability, and empathy, creating a space where both partners feel heard and understood. Recognize that emotional closeness is a dynamic process that evolves over time, needing continual effort and dedication.

Open and Honest Communication

Effective communication is the cornerstone of emotional connection. Create a secure atmosphere for open and honest discussion, where both parties can express their thoughts without fear of judgment. Share your views, dreams, and concerns regularly, actively listening to your partner's perspective
. Through conversation, you develop a bridge of understanding that improves the emotional tie between you and your partner.

Cultivating Empathy

Cultivate empathy by actively seeking to comprehend their experiences, viewpoints, and feelings.

Put yourself in their place, recognizing their feelings even if you may not entirely comprehend them.

By exhibiting empathy, you develop a foundation of emotional support that increases intimacy and connection in your marriage.

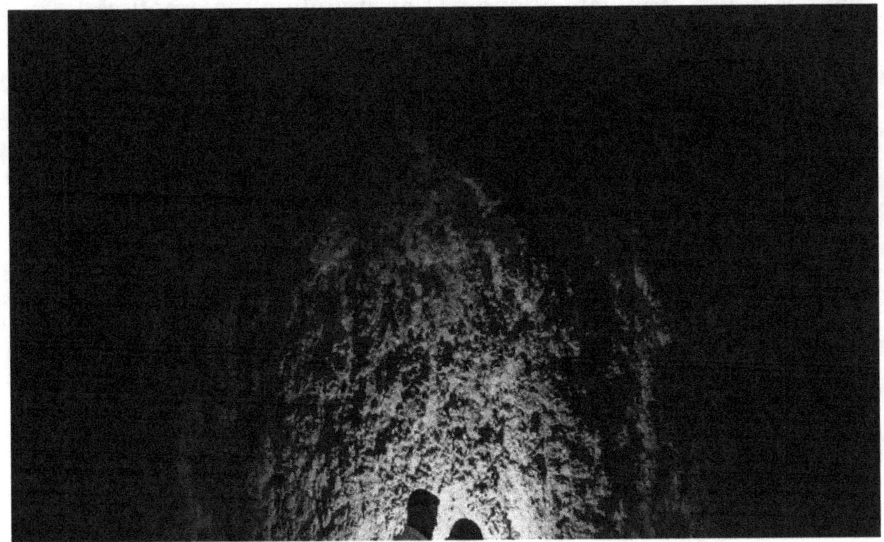

Quality Time and Presence

In the hustle and bustle of daily life, taking out quality time for your partner is vital for creating emotional connection.

Be fully present during these moments, putting away distractions and engaging in meaningful interactions.

Whether it's a private meal, a weekend getaway, or a simple walk together, these moments of connection maintain the emotional closeness between partners.

Shared Experiences and Adventures

Create enduring memories and deepen emotional relationships by sharing experiences and adventures together.

Whether it's discovering new interests, traveling to new locations, or taking on challenges as a team, shared experiences contribute to the story of your partnership. These shared memories become the glue that ties you and your companion, producing a sense of unity and camaraderie.

Prioritizing Emotional Intimacy in the Bedroom

Physical closeness is a fundamental part of emotional connection. Prioritize the intimate element of your relationship by exploring each other's desires, showing affection, and maintaining a healthy and enjoyable sex life. Open discussion about physical intimacy creates a deeper knowledge of each other's needs, adding to the overall emotional well-being of your marriage.

Weathering Challenges Together

Life is packed with hardships that can either bring couples closer or drive them apart. Facing adversities as a united front strengthens resilience and fortifies emotional connection.

Instead of perceiving challenges as hurdles, see them as chances to grow together, supporting each other through thick and thin.

The common experience of conquering problems improves the emotional connection in your marriage.

Seeking Professional Guidance

If emotional closeness in your marriage suffers recurrent issues, seeking expert advice is a proactive step toward resolution. Marriage counselors or therapists can provide tools and tactics to strengthen communication, repair trust, and reignite emotional closeness. Professional support displays a dedication to the health and durability of your partnership.

A Lifelong Commitment to Emotional Connection

Rekindling the love in your marriage through emotional intimacy is a journey that involves time, effort, and attention from both spouses. By applying these tactics, couples can build the emotional tie that forms the cornerstone of their relationship.

Remember, the secrets to a happy marriage lie in the shared experiences, open communication, and the continual dedication to creating and maintaining emotional closeness.

It's a trip worth taking for the long-lasting happiness and fulfillment of your marriage.

CHAPTER FIVE
HEALING FROM BETRAYAL

Betrayal, in whatever form, can be a devastating blow to the core of a partnership. Whether it's infidelity, lost trust, or other forms of betrayal, the aftermath frequently leaves individuals coping with a spectrum of unpleasant feelings.

However, the route towards healing is achievable.

This comprehensive book covers the intricate process of recovering from betrayal, offering practical techniques to rekindle the love and develop a stronger, more resilient relationship.

Acknowledging the Pain

The first step in healing from betrayal is admitting the hurt and allowing yourself to experience the spectrum of emotions that come with it. Understand that healing is a process, and it's okay to experience anger, sadness, uncertainty, and even denial.

Give yourself the room and time to handle these emotions without judgment.

Open and Honest Communication

Effective communication is vital for healing.

Both parties must be willing to engage in open and honest conversations about the betrayal.

Establishing a safe space where feelings can be communicated without fear of judgment is vital.

Discuss the events leading to the betrayal, share your emotions, and attentively listen to your partner's side.

Rebuilding Trust

Rebuilding trust is a gradual process that demands commitment from both parties. Define clear expectations and boundaries moving forward. Consistency in behavior, honesty, and a real effort to reestablish confidence are crucial.

Understand that trust is earned over time, and tiny, consistent actions can contribute considerably to its restoration.

Seeking Professional Support

Healing from betrayal typically entails obtaining professional care. Marriage counselors or therapists can provide a neutral and supportive setting where both couples can express their thoughts, negotiate complex emotions, and learn effective communication and coping methods. Professional counsel can be a key component of the recovery journey.

Cultivating Self-Compassion

Betrayal can lead to feelings of guilt and self-blame. Cultivating self-compassion is vital in the healing process. Understand that no one is flawless, and mistakes happen. Practice self-forgiveness and focus on personal improvement. Building resilience within yourself contributes to the overall strength of the partnership.

Establishing Boundaries

After betrayal, it's vital to establish clear and healthy boundaries. Discuss and clarify what is acceptable and unacceptable behavior in the relationship. Setting limits not only defends against future betrayal but also generates a sense of security and trust between partners.

Rediscovering Intimacy

Rekindling love after betrayal takes regaining closeness. Take the time to rebuild emotional and physical connection gradually. Engage in activities that create connection and closeness. Understand that rebuilding closeness is a collaborative effort and may need time and understanding from both partners.

Embracing Growth and Transformation

Healing from betrayal can be an opportunity for personal and relational improvement. Use the event as a spark for positive transformation. Both couples can learn from the past, practice healthy communication patterns, and gain a deeper knowledge of each other. Embrace the process of growth and evolution as a pair.

A New Chapter of Love and Resilience

Healing from betrayal is a tough but transformative path.

By addressing the grief, encouraging open communication, restoring trust, getting professional treatment, growing self-compassion, creating boundaries, rediscovering intimacy, and accepting change, couples can traverse the path toward rekindling love. The process involves dedication, patience, and a shared vision for a healthier, more resilient partnership.

With devotion and effort, mending is not only possible but may open the door for a new chapter of love and understanding.

INFIDELITY AND TRUST ISSUES

Infidelity is a serious violation that can break the roots of trust within a partnership.

Rebuilding from such an emotional earthquake is a tough challenge, but it's not insurmountable.

This detailed guide digs into the delicate process of healing from infidelity, offering practical techniques to rekindle the love and walk the complicated route towards regaining trust.

Facing the Reality of Infidelity

Acknowledging the fact of adultery is the first step towards healing. Both spouses must confront the hurt, betrayal, and the complicated emotions that arise. It's necessary to have open, honest, and empathetic conversations to grasp the circumstances and the impact of the betrayal on both persons.

Creating a Safe Space for Communication

Effective communication is crucial in the aftermath of infidelity. Establishing a safe space where both partners may share their feelings, worries, and viewpoints without fear of judgment is vital. Encourage honesty and transparency, allowing for a greater understanding of the underlying issues that may have contributed to the adultery.

Rebuilding Trust Brick by Brick

Rebuilding trust is a long process that involves time, consistency, and real effort from both partners.

Establish clear expectations and boundaries moving forward, and commit to rebuilding trust through actions, not just words.

Small, persistent gestures of honesty and reliability become the building blocks for restoring a foundation of confidence.

Seeking Professional Guidance

Navigating the complications of infidelity often benefits from the guidance of a skilled specialist. Marriage counselors or therapists can provide a neutral and supportive setting, offering skills and tactics to facilitate communication, address underlying difficulties, and aid the healing process.

Professional counsel can lend an objective perspective to the complicated emotions involved.

Rebuilding Intimacy

Rekindling love after adultery includes the delicate work of recreating closeness. Both emotional and physical closeness may be harmed, and it's vital to approach the rebuilding process with care and understanding.

Engage in activities that encourage connection, prioritize quality time together, and be open to finding new ways to reconnect and nurture closeness.

Fostering Accountability and Transparency

The partner who engaged in adultery must take responsibility for their conduct and actively strive towards regaining trust.

This requires being accountable, upfront, and open about their locations, actions, and objectives.

Transparency becomes a critical part in maintaining a sense of comfort and predictability in the relationship.

Establishing New Relationship Norms

Rebuilding from infidelity frequently includes a rethinking of partnership rules and expectations.

Both partners should be willing to talk and establish new boundaries that foster a better and more secure interaction.

This approach requires a mutual commitment to create a relational climate that encourages growth, understanding, and emotional safety.

Embracing Personal Growth

Infidelity can be a chance for personal growth and self-reflection. Both couples should take the time to assess their respective needs, values, and objectives. Embracing personal growth can lead to a better sense of self and, subsequently, a more resilient and meaningful relationship.

A Journey Towards Renewed Love and Trust

Healing after infidelity is a nuanced and demanding road that requires commitment, patience, and a willingness to address uncomfortable truths.

By addressing the truth of infidelity, creating a safe space for conversation, restoring trust, obtaining professional help, cultivating intimacy, promoting accountability, establishing new marital rules, and embracing personal growth, couples can traverse the route towards rekindling love.

The process is tough, but with devotion and effort, it can lead to a renewed sense of connection, trust, and a more profound, durable love.

KEEP
YOUR
HEAD
UP

REBUILDING TRUST

Trust is the cornerstone of any flourishing relationship, and when it's undermined, the journey to restore can be both tough and transformative. This comprehensive book explores the delicate yet powerful process of restoring trust, offering practical techniques to rekindle the love and establish a stronger, more resilient relationship.

Acknowledging the Trust Deficit

The first step in rebuilding trust is acknowledging the problem. Both partners need to identify and confront the breach honestly, establishing a space for open communication about the hurt, feelings, and repercussions related with the broken trust.

Open and Honest Dialogue

Effective communication forms the bedrock of trust rebuilding. Establish an environment where both parties feel safe expressing their feelings, worries, and expectations without fear of judgment. This discourse should be characterized by active listening, empathy, and a dedication to understanding each other's viewpoints.

HOW TO FIGHT FOR YOUR MARRIAGE

Consistency in Actions

Consistency is key in rebuilding trust. Trust is not simply about promises but about consistent actions that fit with those commitments. Small, good behaviors over time can gradually rebuild a sense of reliability and security, indicating that trust can be rebuilt.

Establishing Clear Boundaries

Setting clear limits is vital for rebuilding trust.
Both spouses should actively participate in setting acceptable actions and expectations. Clearly established limits create a framework for respect and understanding, helping to prevent future trust concerns.

Patience and Understanding

Rebuilding trust is a process that requires time and understanding. Both parties should know that mending takes time, and hurrying the process can harm development. Patience enables for a steady development of trust through persistent positive actions and behaviors.

Accountability and Apology

For the party responsible for the breach, taking accountability is vital. A heartfelt apology, coupled with a genuine resolve to change, is a powerful step in regaining trust.
Demonstrating sincere sorrow and comprehending the impact of one's conduct is vital for the healing process.

Seeking Professional Support

In more difficult circumstances, seeking professional advice might be beneficial. Marriage counselors or therapists can give significant insights, communication techniques, and tactics customized to the individual needs of the couple.
Professional help provides a neutral space for both spouses to communicate issues and facilitates a guided approach toward regaining trust.

Rebuilding Self-Trust

Rebuilding trust within the relationship typically includes rebuilding trust in oneself. Individuals may need to reflect on their values, priorities, and personal progress.

By working on self-trust, individuals contribute greatly to the whole trust-building process inside the partnership.

A Renewed Foundation for Love

Rebuilding trust is a tough yet rewarding endeavor that may breathe new life into a relationship.

By acknowledging the trust deficit, fostering open communication, prioritizing consistency, setting clear boundaries, practicing patience and understanding, taking accountability, seeking professional support when needed, and rebuilding self-trust, couples can embark on a path toward a renewed foundation for love. Trust, once destroyed, may be repaired with devotion, empathy, and a mutual commitment to rekindling the love that links them together.

CHAPTER SIX

FIGHTING FOR YOUR MARRIAGE

While marriage is a union of love and devotion, it frequently experiences problems that necessitate a resilient and proactive approach. This thorough guide is intended to provide couples with practical tactics and insights for fighting for their marriage, reigniting the flames of love, and rediscovering the magic that brought them together.

Recognizing Obstacles

Recognizing the issues is the first step in fighting for your marriage. The cornerstone for comprehending the issues at hand and working together toward solutions is honest self-reflection and open discussion between partners about the difficulties they experience.

Communication Skills

A successful marriage is built on effective communication. Learn and practice active listening, openly share your thoughts and feelings, and create a secure environment for your partner to do the same. Transparent and compassionate communication fosters connection and togetherness by creating a bridge of understanding.

Making Quality Time a Priority

Couples can easily lose sight of each other in the hustle and bustle of daily life. Prioritize quality time together to rekindle the relationship. Whether it's a weekly date night, a weekend vacation, or simply a peaceful evening at home, these occasions foster connection and intimacy.

Intimacy Nurturing

Physical and emotional connection are essential components of a happy marriage. Take deliberate steps to cultivate both elements of intimacy. Investigate each other's desires, be open to new experiences, and prioritize affection.
A healthy intimate relationship adds greatly to your marriage's overall well-being.

Setting and Achieving Shared Objectives

Setting and achieving agreed goals is part of fighting for your marriage. Collaborate with your partner to find shared goals and envision your future together. This common goal enhances your bond and serves as a road map for the future.

Resilience in the Face of Adversity

Marriage frequently faces external and internal problems.
Cultivate resilience as a couple by experiencing hardships together.
Consider challenges as opportunities for growth and learning, and
devise solutions for navigating them together.
Resilience is the foundation of a marriage that will stand the test of
time.

Seeking Professional Help

Seeking expert help when issues get overwhelming is a proactive
step in fighting for your marriage.
Marriage counselors or therapists can offer essential insights,
communication techniques, and tactics geared to your particular
dynamics. Professional assistance provides a safe area for both
spouses to share their problems and work toward solutions.

Rediscovering One Another

Couples may grow independently over time, and the key to
rekindling love is rediscovering each other.
Spend some time getting to know your partner's current interests,
dreams, and objectives. Create shared experiences that allow you
to grow as individuals while also strengthening your relationship
as a pair.

A Renewing Commitment to Love

Fighting for your marriage is actively participating in the process of growth and regeneration rather than avoiding confrontation. Couples can embark on a journey to rediscover each other by acknowledging challenges, practicing effective communication, prioritizing quality time, nurturing intimacy, setting shared goals, embracing resilience, seeking professional guidance when needed, and rediscovering each other. It is a pledge to a shared future filled with love, understanding, and a renewed enthusiasm for the adventure of marriage.

PRACTICAL STRATEGIES TO OVERCOME TOUGH TIMES

Tough times are an unavoidable part of the delicate dance of love and partnership. The capacity to manage obstacles together not only enhances a relationship's basis but also allows for growth, resilience, and a deeper connection.

This comprehensive guide delves into practical ways for overcoming adversity, providing couples with tangible insights for rekindling the love and emerging from adversity with a renewed dedication to each other.

Recognizing Difficulties

Recognizing and comprehending difficult times is the first step in overcoming them. Recognizing the issues at hand is critical, whether they are external pressures, individual hardships, or unforeseen calamities. Partners must approach difficult times as a team, perceiving them as chances for progress rather than insurmountable obstacles.

FIGHT
FOR
YOUR
RIGHT

Communication Skills

A sustainable relationship is built on open and honest communication. It is much more important during difficult times. Create a nonjudgmental environment in which to share your thoughts, feelings, and worries.

Actively listen to one another, validate emotions, and avoid laying blame. Effective communication creates understanding, establishes trust, and lays the framework for collaborative problem solving.

Mutual Aid and Collaboration

Dealing with adversity as a group builds a strong support system. Develop mutual support by actively participating in each other's challenges. Encourage one another, share duties, and rejoice in tiny wins together. The sense of belonging to a united front enhances the relationship and supports the idea that you are all in this together.

Making Self-Care a Priority

Individuals must prioritize self-care during difficult circumstances. Encourage one another to participate in activities that improve mental, emotional, and physical health.

A dedication to self-care, whether through regular exercise, mindfulness techniques, or the pursuit of personal hobbies, contributes to a healthier, more resilient individual, which enhances the relationship.

Establishing Reasonable Expectations

Tough circumstances can strain a relationship, so it's critical to set realistic expectations. Be truthful about how much each spouse can reasonably offer given the circumstances.

Recognize that perfection is not the aim; instead, concentrate on development and collaborative efforts. Setting attainable goals offers a sense of accomplishment while avoiding undue stress.

Seeking Professional Advice

Seeking expert help when the issues seem overwhelming is a proactive and planned step.

Relationship counselors or therapists can offer couples objective advice, insightful insights, and effective communication methods and coping mechanisms. Professional assistance provides a safe area for both spouses to share issues and collaborate on solutions.

Concentrating on Common Goals

During difficult times, refocusing attention on common goals can provide a sense of purpose and solidarity. Identify short-term and long-term goals that are in line with your values and aspirations as a marriage. Focusing on common goals strengthens your commitment to the relationship, whether it's planning a future together, pursuing a shared passion, or handling a challenging situation as a team.

KEEP
YOUR
HEAD
UP

Embracing Adaptability and Flexibility

When it comes to overcoming adversity, flexibility and adaptation are essential. Life is unpredictably unpredictable, and the capacity to adjust plans and expectations aids in navigating obstacles with a more resilient perspective. Accept change as a chance for growth and evolution, and approach difficult times with a flexible mindset that allows for modifications in response to ever-changing circumstances.

Developing Resilience in the Face of Adversity

Adversity is a natural part of life, and developing resilience in the face of adversity is essential for a long-lasting relationship. Rather than seeing problems as defeats, consider them opportunities for personal and relational growth. The ability to recover from hardship, learn from experiences, and emerge stronger is referred to as resilience. Face problems head on, learn from setbacks, and adjust to the changing dynamics of your relationship to build resilience.

A Renewing Commitment to Love and Resilience

Overcoming adversity is much more than simply surviving; it's about thriving as a relationship. Couples can rekindle the love that brought them together by understanding the challenges, practicing effective communication, providing mutual support, prioritizing self-care, setting realistic expectations, seeking professional guidance when needed, focusing on shared goals, embracing flexibility, and building resilience through adversity.

When accompanied by dedication and practical techniques, the journey through difficult times has the ability to alter a relationship, resulting in a stronger, more robust, and more linked couple.

THE BENEFITS OF CONSIDERING MARRIAGE COUNSELING

Marriage is a journey filled with joy, friendship, and shared ambitions, but it also comes with its fair share of obstacles.

When couples find themselves facing problems that appear insurmountable, marital counseling emerges as a strong tool to traverse the intricacies of relationships.

This comprehensive book digs into the benefits of seeking marriage counseling, presenting insights into how it may be a transforming step towards rekindling the love and cementing the tie between spouses.

Acknowledging the Need for Support

The decision to seek marriage counseling generally begins with identifying the need for support.

Challenges such as communication breakdowns, unresolved disputes, or external stressors might strain the partnership.

Recognizing that external assistance may be valuable displays a commitment to the health and longevity of the partnership.

A Neutral and Safe Environment

One of the key benefits of marriage counseling is the formation of a neutral and safe environment. In this area, both partners can share their thoughts, feelings, and worries without fear of condemnation.

The counselor works as a neutral third party, allowing open conversation and providing insights that help unravel the difficulties of the relationship.

Improved Communication Skills

Effective communication is the bedrock of a healthy relationship. Marriage counseling equips couples with vital communication skills, teaching them how to express themselves more effectively, actively listen to each other, and handle challenging talks.

These qualities encourage understanding, empathy, and a deeper connection between partners.

Resolving Unresolved Issues

Many couples attend counseling with unresolved difficulties that remain beneath the surface.

These unaddressed conflicts can provide a growing ground for bitterness and dissatisfaction. Marriage counseling provides a systematic platform for discussing and resolving these remaining difficulties, allowing couples to go ahead with a clear slate.

Strengthening Emotional Intimacy

Emotional intimacy is the glue that binds couples together. Marriage counseling helps partners explore and deepen their emotional connection.

By cultivating vulnerability, empathy, and mutual understanding, couples can reestablish the emotional connection that may have deteriorated over time.

Developing Conflict Resolution Strategies

Every relationship has challenges, but it's how couples handle and resolve these disputes that determine the strength of the connection. Marriage counseling delivers effective conflict resolution skills, helping couples to handle differences constructively and discover common ground without escalating tensions.

Rekindling Intimacy and Connection

Physical intimacy is a fundamental part of a love relationship. Over time, things such as stress, communication failures, or unresolved difficulties can hinder intimacy.

Marriage counseling gives a platform to address these difficulties, offering couples methods to reestablish physical connection and reignite the flame in their relationship.

Clarifying Relationship Expectations

Misaligned expectations can lead to misunderstandings and disappointment. Marriage counseling encourages conversations around each partner's expectations, helping to clarify and align them. When both individuals have a good grasp of what the other expects, it decreases the possibility of disappointed expectations becoming sources of conflict.

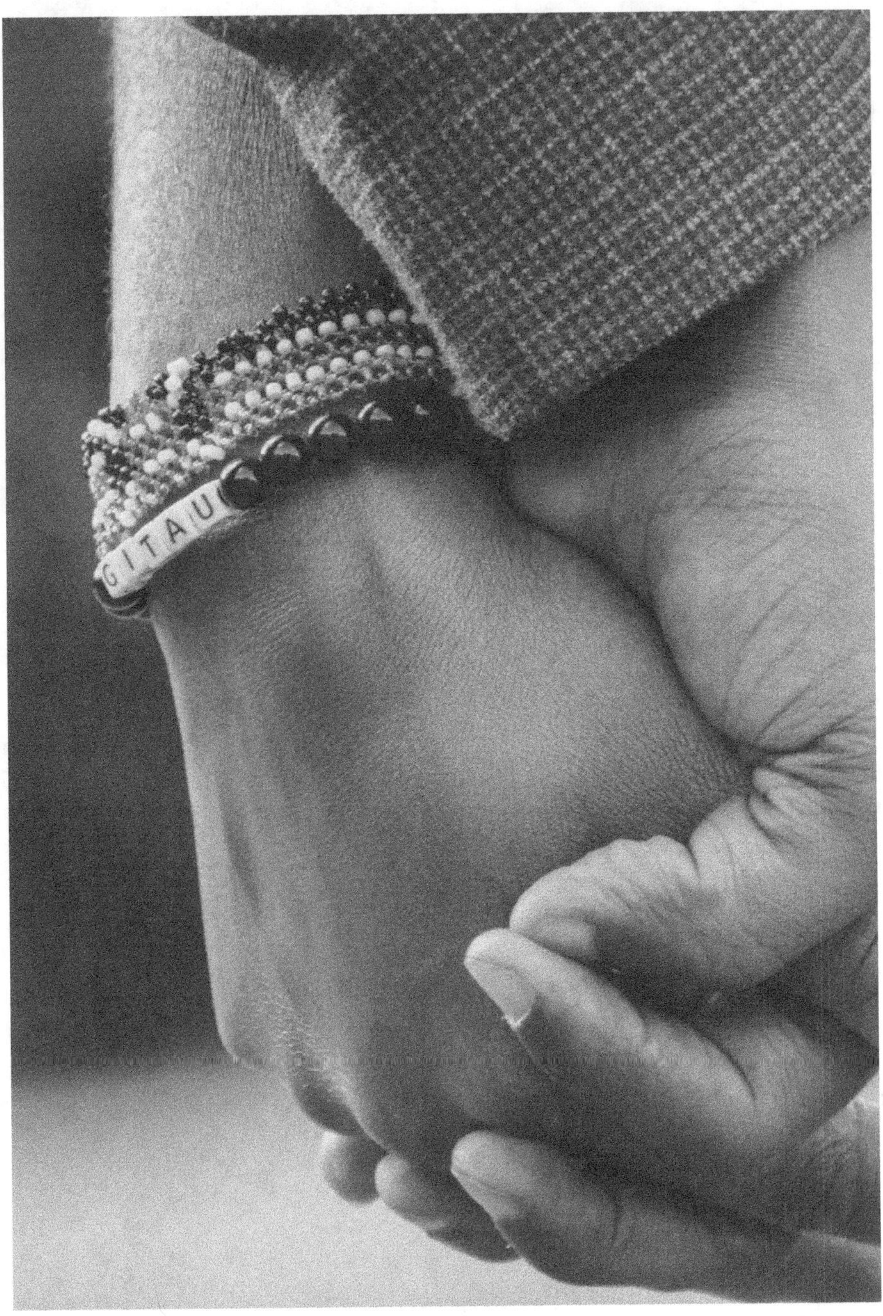

Navigating Major Life Transitions

Major life adjustments, such as work shifts, becoming parents, or dealing with empty nest syndrome, can substantially damage a relationship. Marriage counseling provides direction and support during these transitions, helping couples navigate the changes and adjust to new dynamics in their partnership.

Encouraging Individual Growth

A healthy marriage needs two persons committed to personal improvement. Marriage counseling recognizes the importance of individual well-being and encourages spouses to explore personal improvement within the context of the relationship.
This emphasis on individual progress contributes to the overall strength of the relationship.

Revitalizing a Stale Relationship

Couples may find themselves in a rut when the relationship feels boring or uninspiring. Marriage counseling brings techniques to pump new energy into the partnership, creating creativity, shared experiences, and a renewed sense of excitement about the future together.

Strengthening the Commitment

Marriage counseling reinforces the commitment between spouses. By putting time and effort into counseling, couples display a shared passion to the relationship's success.

This commitment can act as a tremendous motivator for overcoming problems and developing a resilient partnership.

A Renewed and Resilient Relationship

In the search of a lasting and meaningful marriage, the decision to explore marriage therapy is a proactive step towards developing a fresh and robust connection.

By acknowledging the need for support, creating a neutral and safe environment, improving communication skills, resolving unresolved issues, strengthening emotional intimacy, developing conflict resolution strategies, rekindling intimacy and connection, clarifying relationship expectations, navigating major life transitions, encouraging individual growth, and revitalizing a stale relationship, couples can unlock the full spectrum of benefits that marriage counseling offers. It is a path towards rekindling the love and developing a connection that stands the test of time.

CONCLUSION

Undertaking the endeavor to revive the affection and reinforce your marital bond is a deep-seated commitment that needs unwavering devotion, exertion, and a methodical technique.

In this extensive book, we have examined several undisclosed information, tactics, and practical measures to effectively traverse the intricacies of marriage.

As we get to the end, it is crucial to integrate these observations and highlight the profound impact of using these tactics in the pursuit of a durable and satisfying relationship.

Contemplating the Secrets Guide

Recognizing The need For Transformation

The first and maybe the most essential stage in the Secrets Guide is recognizing the need for alteration.

Acknowledging that every partnership has difficulties and actively striving to find solutions paves the road for development and rejuvenation.

Communication as a Fundamental Basis

The guide consistently emphasized the need of effective communication. It is the cornerstone of a good relationship. Through cultivating transparent, sincere, and compassionate dialogue, partners establish a basis for comprehension, bonding, and the settlement of disagreements.

Building and Rebuilding Trust

Trust, once damaged, needs purposeful efforts to repair. Strategies such as establishing clear limits, exercising consistency, and obtaining professional help contribute to the gradual restoration of trust. Trust is not only necessary for a good relationship but is also the cornerstone upon which love may thrive.

Rediscovering Emotional and Physical Intimacy

Emotional and physical connection are the lifeblood of a love relationship. The guide highlighted the significance of rediscovering and strengthening both qualities.
From growing self-compassion to putting aside meaningful time for shared activities, the route to reignite love entails consciously creating closeness.

Navigating the Complexities of Infidelity

The guide went into the delicate process of recovering after infidelity. Strategies like as open communication, responsibility, and developing new relationship rules are crucial components in overcoming the enormous obstacles provided by betrayal.

Healing is possible, and with dedication, couples may create a stronger, more resilient relationship.

As we complete the book, it's vital to underline the necessity of seeing the offered tactics not as separate stages but as interwoven components of a holistic approach to marriage.

Rekindling the love and fighting for your marriage is a continual struggle, and the real strength resides in the persistent use of these tactics over time.

Commitment to Continuous Growth

A good marriage is not static; it is a growing organism that demands ongoing development and change.

Couples are taught to perceive obstacles not as impediments but as opportunities for personal and relationship growth.

Embrace the concept that progress is a shared journey.

Resilience in the Face of Challenges

The Secrets Guide highlights the necessity for resilience when dealing with adversities. Life is unpredictable, and terrible times are unavoidable. Couples are taught to handle obstacles with a spirit of resilience, perceiving them not as threats but as chances to improve their partnership.

Professional Support as a Catalyst

Seeking professional help emerged as a strong motivator for progress. Marriage counselors or therapists give useful insights, impartial viewpoints, and specialized techniques to handle challenging challenges.
Couples are urged to break down the stigma associated with requesting assistance and embrace professional counsel as a proactive step towards a healthy relationship.

Celebrating Small Victories

In the quest to reignite love, appreciating tiny wins is crucial. Every good move, no matter how tiny, adds to the total growth. Couples should acknowledge and enjoy moments of connection, successful communication, and mutual understanding.

The Ongoing Pursuit of Connection

Rekindling love is not a one-time occurrence but a continual endeavor. The handbook urges couples to focus and constantly invest in their relationship.

Whether via shared hobbies, quality time, or purposeful gestures of love, the continual desire of connection is important to a happy marriage.

A Vision for the Future

In the end of the Secrets Guide, couples are urged to picture the future they desire to build together.

A future based on a foundation of love, trust, good communication, and resilience. It's a future where problems are confronted together, progress is welcomed, and the relationship between couples develops with each passing day.

Rekindling the love and fighting for your marriage is a brave and transforming process.

It needs self-reflection, honest communication, and a commitment to improvement.

By accepting the tactics suggested in this book and seeing them as part of a holistic strategy, couples may traverse the intricacies of marriage with resilience, fortitude, and a shared vision for a future filled with love, understanding, and lasting connection.

The Secrets Guide is not just a guidebook; it's an invitation to go on a journey of regeneration, development, and the rediscovery of a love that stands the test of time.